Changing Direction

Direction

Employment options in mid-life

Sue Ward

ACE BOOKS

ꭗ

© 1996 Sue Ward
Published by Age Concern England
1268 London Road
London SW16 4ER

Editor Caroline Hartnell
Design and production Eugenie Dodd Typographics
Copy preparation Vinnette Marshall
Printed and bound in Great Britain by J W Arrowsmith Ltd, Bristol

A catalogue record for this book is available
from the British Library.

ISBN 0–86242–190–X

Contents

About the author

Sue Ward is a freelance journalist and researcher specialising in pensions and social security matters. She has regular commitments teaching about occupational pensions and social security. She has also carried out advisory work for the Equal Opportunities Commission on equal treatment in pensions.

Her publications include: *The Pensions Handbook*, ACE Books, published annually; *Essential Guide to Pensions*, Pluto Press, 1992 (third edition); *Managing the Pensions Revolution*, Nicholas Brealey Publishing, 1995; *Women and Personal Pensions* (jointly with Bryn Davies), HMSO for Equal Opportunities Commission, 1992. She is also the author of regular articles in national newspapers and in specialist magazines such as *Pensions World* and *Pensions Management*.

She was a member of the Government-appointed Pensions Law Review Committee (the Goode Committee), reviewing the framework of pensions law and regulation, in 1992–93.

Acknowledgements

My thanks to all those who have helped me with the preparation of this book, and to everyone from whose experience I have quoted. I have had extensive conversations with many people, especially here on Tyneside where I live. In this region we do have unrivalled experience of suffering job loss, and a great many resilient people who have fought back and taken a positive attitude.

Special thanks for our very helpful discussions to Dot Kirton, Linda Aitken, Sheila March, Marilyn Headley, and Brian Cooper of Coutts Career Consultants; Susan Wass and Deborah Knox of Tyneside TEC; Jennifer Hills and Eileen Ridley of the Employment Service in Wallsend; Libby Hinson of Gateshead CAB; Betty Hill, and Margaret McPhail of Tyneside Careers.

Thanks also to the Institute of Personnel and Development, and the Press Offices of the Department of Social Security and Department of Employment (as it was then) for dealing with my queries, and to the Inland Revenue for supplying me with material on the taxation of redundancy payments. Any opinions, of course, are entirely my own.

Sue Ward
August 1995

Introduction

So it has finally happened: your job is coming to an end. The news may have been a bolt from the blue, or it may have been long expected. There may have been rumours of an announcement over several weeks or months, or an early retirement or redundancy package on offer for some time, which you have decided to take. You may even have chosen to take the initiative yourself, if the working conditions no longer suit you. Like many other people today, you may be feeling that you are stale in your job and have given all you have to give, but have come across nothing that would suit you better. Peter, an adult education tutor, feels this way:

'This isn't a job you can go on doing for ever, because you run out of ideas. I look at the job advertisements but there never seems to be anything good. I may well be made redundant with the way things are going, and I suppose that would give me the push I really need.'

This book is aimed at people in their 40s or 50s. It is slanted towards those taking redundancy, but should be useful for anyone whose previous employment has finished, but who is not ready to sit back and watch the garden grow, even if they have the money to do so.

If you are in this age group, you will have lots of experience of work and of how the world works, even if you have no formal qualifications, or only ones that you feel are out of date.

For anyone, a change of this sort is a major upheaval. It is only natural to feel anxious about where you start. This book is intended to guide you through the possibilities, looking much wider than the 'standard' full-time, nine-to-five job (which is far from standard any more anyway). It covers the possibilities – and pitfalls – of working full-time or part-time, setting up on your own, working as a volunteer, retraining or going back into education, or mixing all of these in a 'portfolio' of activities.

It is aimed both at those who do want to carry on in the same direction as before – the same sort of job package, in the same field – and at those who want (or feel they need) to strike out in a different direction.

For both groups, there *are* opportunities if you look for them. You'll find them more easily, and probably find them more rewarding, if you

▶ know what you want to do;

▶ plan and research how you are going to do it;

▶ treat getting there as a serious project in its own right.

For many people, this will be a quite different approach from the one you took when you were last looking for a job – which may be two or three decades ago when there was full employment. Youngsters then tended to drift into what seemed the most attractive opportunity at the time, without thinking too much about a 'career path'. Or they took something as a stopgap till 'something better comes up' and are still there. This time round it's different. There is the chance – and the need – to organise things properly. There are also new constraints. The aim of this book is to help you deal with these successfully.

CHAPTER ONE

Your feelings about losing your job

Losing your job is never good news. You have had a settled environment, where you know people and understand how the system works. Now you are faced with all sorts of uncertainties.

However well they think they are prepared, when the break comes many people feel

▸ hurt and undervalued;

▸ angry;

▸ lacking in confidence.

Even if you volunteered for redundancy or early retirement, you may still have felt pressure to go. There are some employers who are very unsubtle about this. People are sometimes offered redeployments which it is known would be unacceptable, or have heavy hints dropped about 'leaving the jobs for younger people'.

Hopefully your employer has not behaved like this, but you may have felt that you had to take a decision more quickly than you wanted. Often it is stressed that the early retirement or redundancy package being provided is on offer only for a limited time, and that any future redundancies will be on worse terms.

Feeling rejected and lacking in confidence

So it is only natural that you will feel angry and hurt about what is happening. The very word 'redundancy' carries with it an implication that you are rejected, unwanted. If you feel that you have been doing a good job for your employer, this is humiliating and may cast a shadow over all that you have achieved in the past. The employer may have looked for commitment and loyalty in the past, and you will have responded by identifying yourself with them. So, for example, when someone employed by Marks and Spencer is asked what they do at a party, they are quite likely to reply 'I work for Marks and Spencer', rather than 'I am an accountant' or 'I manage a shop'.

To have that basic framework knocked away can cast doubt on your whole self-image. Often the response is to feel out of control. You knew where you were before, but now you do not.

One outplacement adviser with a large organisation finds that people over 50 show a great sense of rejection when they come to see her, particularly as in most cases they will have spent their whole working lives with the company. While financial issues are an immediate concern, it is usually of more importance how they deal with losing their jobs in terms of the apparent loss of identity, status and ego. In general, she says, men's and women's attitudes to job loss seem to differ, and women find it easier to adjust. This is perhaps because women with family commitments tend quickly to recognise other priorities in their lives.

She also says that people often lack confidence in themselves, feeling that they will never be able to get a job for the same salary elsewhere, or that they have no skills which will be saleable on the open market.

Her particular firm gives a lot of help with finding new jobs (usually called 'outplacement' in the current jargon) for its redundant staff. But both she and others are convinced that the initial stage, of taking stock and deciding what you want to do, is if anything more important. Sitting down and planning, in an organised and structured way, combats the hurt and anger and helps to restore confidence – as well as leading towards the end you are aiming at.

The larger the employer, and the larger the number of people affected, the more likely it is that they will plan any staff reduction programme properly. Firms like BT, British Gas, the banks and Shell have put considerable resources both into counselling and into outplacement services. With a small employer, or when a company unexpectedly goes into receivership, there may be virtually no notice at all.

Even in large firms, it is quite common for employers to tell people who are leaving not to work out their notice periods – either because they feel it will be bad for the morale of other staff or because they fear sabotage or misuse of confidential information once a person no longer feels a loyalty to them. So you may get the 'black plastic bag' treatment – being escorted to your desk where you empty the contents into a plastic bin-liner, handing over your keys to the company car and leaving the premises all within a couple of hours. Don't take it personally. It will be a policy decision at a high level, nothing to do with you.

Talking about your feelings

However it happens, you will always need time and space to adjust. The process that people go through is almost one of grieving. Talk through your feelings with someone who will listen sympathetically, but who is not so partisan that they wind you up further. People trained in counselling and listening skills will be able to do this; family and friends may themselves feel too strongly about what has happened to be very useful.

If your employer is offering a counselling service, it is well worth taking advantage of it. Counselling is available on the NHS, though in short supply, and you could ask your GP for a referral. Otherwise, you could find someone privately (for some possible sources, see the 'Useful addresses' section), talk to a local clergyman, or perhaps ring the Samaritans. They are not there just for people who feel suicidal, but for anyone who needs an ear to bend because they feel despairing in one way or another.

Another possibility is to look for a suitable course or workshop. One organisation, Life Changes, runs one-day and two-day workshops in Bristol. According to the publicity, these aim to help people

- *identify their issues or concerns about major life changes;*
- *identify any blocks or resistance to transition or change;*
- *identify strategies for moving forward; and*
- *develop an appropriate Life Plan for the future.*

There may be a similar organisation near you, or you could find a residential course, perhaps over a weekend. Word of mouth is probably the best way to ensure that it is a reputable course and that your time will not be wasted, so ask around for recommendations.

Many employers and local education authorities offer **mid-life career planning** and **pre-retirement courses**. They are well worth going on but offer something rather different. They provide practical help with issues such as managing your money and keeping in good health; they are aimed more at those who intend to retire fully than at those who want to carry on doing something. But they also offer the space to talk things through and think about the future, so it will be worth taking up the offer of one if it is available. If the course is run within the company, someone from the Pensions Department will almost certainly attend and be able to answer questions about your entitlements.

If you don't give yourself the chance to talk through your feelings, they will fester and could sour your life. Many of the ex-staff she knows, one adviser says, find it almost impossible now to go back into the building where they worked, even for a social occasion, because of the feelings it stirs up. Two and a half years on, she found herself being bearded at a party by an ex-colleague who was vitriolic about her former manager and quite unable to acknowledge that she had had a generous package and special arrangements made.

Taking a break

Whatever your longer-term plans may be, in the short term you probably need a break. Even if you have found work while you are still finishing your notice period, it is still wise to take a break between the end of one job and the beginning of the next. This gives you the time to grieve, and it marks the break between one part of your life and the next. That will help reduce the amount of baggage you carry (the 'When I was at X we did it *this* way' habit) from one to the other. You may also feel stressed with all the pressures of finishing off work and planning for the future.

If you need to go straight on to Unemployment Benefit (or Jobseeker's Allowance after October 1996; see pp 115–118), taking a break is not made easy, but there may well be a few weeks before you are able to sign on in any case – for instance if you have been given a payment in lieu of notice (as explained on pp 29–30).

If you are pessimistic about the future, you may feel anxious about spending any of the redundancy payment or pension lump sum you have taken with you from your last employer. Alternatively, you may feel demob-happy and want to blow the lot, which is equally unwise. It is up to you how much you spend, but you are certainly entitled to invest a sensible proportion of your pay-off in a decent holiday or something you have always wanted to do. Many people take the opportunity to give themselves a longer break than they could have had while in work – perhaps the holiday of a lifetime on the other side of the world. Or you may decide that now is your chance to fulfil a pipedream, like a climbing holiday in Nepal or a trip to Australia to visit relatives there. By all means take the opportunity – it may never come again.

CHAPTER TWO

What you may get at the end of your old job

The early retirement or redundancy package you receive when you leave your job will probably consist of various different elements. The law specifies minimum periods of notice and redundancy payments, but most employers offer considerably more than the legal minimum. This chapter looks at your statutory entitlements and the benefits employers might offer on top of these. It also looks at what happens if you have a personal pension, the tax position, and how State benefits may be affected.

The statutory minimum entitlements

Legal rights in employment are limited and can be difficult to enforce. In general, the entitlements below apply to both full-time workers and (since February 1995) part-timers without any lower limit on hours. See pages 18–19 for suggestions on how to sort out problems that may arise.

Notice periods and time off to look for other work

Many people have a notice period specified in their contract of employment, and this should normally be followed unless *you* agree to waive it. There are minimum notice periods laid down by law. These are:

▶ **By the employee**: 1 week.

▶ **By the employer**, where the continuous period of employment was

–less than 2 years: 1 week;
–between 2 and 12 years: 1 week for each year of continuous
  employment (ie 3 weeks after 3 years' employment);
–12 years or more: 12 weeks.

In the case of redundancies, employers also have a legal duty to consult the trade unions before declaring a redundancy. Where there are to be more than 10 redundancies, there should be at least 30 days' notice; if the number is more than 100, there should be at least 90 days' notice.

If you are asked not to work out your notice, then you will usually be entitled to payment in lieu of notice (see pp 28–31 for details of how this is taxed, and the effect it may have on any social security benefits).

If the employer does not meet the statutory requirements for notice of redundancy (covered above), an industrial tribunal can also give a 'protective award' of up to 90 days' pay.

While working out your notice you are entitled to 'reasonable' time off to seek alternative work or training (under the Trade Union and Labour Relations (Consolidation) Act 1992, clauses 168–170).

Redundancy payments

The law lays down minimum levels of redundancy pay, though many employers offer something considerably better. The minimum is:

▶ one and a half weeks' pay for each year of employment in which you were aged 41 or more;

▶ one week's pay for each year of employment in which you were aged 22–40;

▶ half a week's pay for each year of employment at any age up to 21.

A maximum of 20 years (the last 20 years' service) can be taken into account; the maximum 'pay' for these purposes is £205 per week. So the total statutory maximum is £6,150. Redundancy pay is not payable at all if you are over 65; women between the State retirement age of 60 and 65 must be given the same rights as men of the same age (under the Sex Discrimination Act 1987). In the year before your 65th birthday, statutory redundancy payments are reduced by $\frac{1}{12}$ for every month after the 64th birthday.

The pension offset

Redundancy pay can in certain cases be offset against money coming from your pension scheme. If the annual value of the pension is a third or more of your annual pay, then the right to a statutory redundancy payment may be lost altogether. If it is less than a third of your annual pay, the redundancy payment can be reduced. These rules apply only where the pension is coming into payment immediately, or quite soon.

It is, however, very rare for employers to make use of these rules in order to cut back on the statutory redundancy payment. As explained on pages 22–23, they are more likely to offer a trade-off between different forms of additional payment.

Enforcing your legal rights

Employers, especially small ones, may not understand the legal position, or they may be unwilling to fulfil their obligations. It is not always clear when a job loss is counted as a redundancy, and you may need to dispute this. If you think your employer has got things wrong, and you are a member of a trade union or staff association, go to them with any problems. Alternatively, you could ask the Government advisory service ACAS (see 'Useful addresses') to explain to them what your rights are, and possibly to take enforcement action.

If your firm has gone into liquidation or receivership, and there is not enough left to pay the redundancy payments, then the statutory level of redundancy pay can be claimed from the National Insurance Fund. In these circumstances you will *certainly* need the help of a trade union or staff association, ACAS, or a solicitor. You will probably save time and money if all those affected work as a group, rather than each doing their own thing.

Since the reorganisation of Government departments, redundancy is dealt with by the Department of Trade and Industry. But their free leaflet explaining the position (PL 808; see 'Useful publications') is still available from Jobcentres as well as CABs and libraries. There is also a free helpline and information unit on redundancy (see 'Useful addresses').

See Lynda Macdonald's book *Hired, Fired, or Sick and Tired* for details of the law covering this whole area and how to enforce your rights.

Packages better than the legal minimum

Where employers want to reduce staffing without damaging the organisation, they may offer generous terms to employees who are willing to go. There are two elements to this: redundancy (or severance) pay, and early retirement pension and lump sum under the employer's pension scheme.

Redundancy/severance pay

Most larger employers give more than the legal minimum for redundancy or severance, at least for longer-serving staff. One 1995 survey, carried out by Industrial Relations Services for their journal *Employment Trends*, found that out of 50 organisations surveyed, 45 made extra payments; 44 per cent of employers included contractual allowances in the calculation, and 36 per cent included performance-related payments. Over 90 per cent treated part-time service in the same way as full-time service (pro rata) and included periods of long-term sickness and paid and unpaid maternity leave in determining the period of qualifying service. Many disregarded the statutory ceiling on pay of £205 a week.

To take a couple of examples from the survey, Glory Mills Papers gave four weeks' pay for each complete year of service, while GEC-Marconi gave 2 per cent of annual salary for each year of service, on top of the statutory payment.

Your employer's pension

What pension entitlement you have will depend on:

▶ your age;
▶ the legal rules enforced by the Inland Revenue and the DSS;
▶ the provisions of the scheme;
▶ the willingness of the employer or trustees to top up your pension.

NOTE   This book is not going into detail on pensions, because there is so much else to cover. For information on the legal position, and how pension schemes are set up and run, see *The Pensions Handbook*, published annually by ACE Books.

If you have been in the scheme under two years

If you have been only a very short time in an employer's pension scheme, under two years, you are likely to receive a partial refund of your contributions. Around half, possibly even less, will come back to you; the rest will go to the Department of Social Security to buy you back into the State Earnings-Related Pension Scheme (SERPS) and to the Inland Revenue as tax.

If you are under 50

If you have been in the scheme longer than two years but are under the age of 50, then you will be able to draw a pension only if you are suffering from ill-health. According to the Inland Revenue definition, this means:

'physical or mental deterioration which is sufficiently serious to prevent the individual from following his or her normal employment, or which seriously impairs his or her earning capacity. It does not mean simply a decline in earning capacity.'

Within this definition, some schemes define ill-health as meaning inability to do your own job or a similar one; others define it as inability to do *any* job. It could be the employer, the company doctor or the trustees who decide whether you qualify. Check in your own scheme rules.

If you do not qualify under the ill-health rules, then if you are aged under 50 you will be entitled to a **deferred pension**, which you have a right to transfer elsewhere if you wish. (Transferring is frequently not a good idea; see ACE Books annual publication *The Pensions Handbook* for more information.) This must be increased each year until you draw it. Under many schemes' rules, you will be able to start drawing your pension at any age from 50 onwards, but at a much reduced rate.

If you are 50 or over

If you are 50 or over (or sometimes 55), in most schemes you will be able to draw an early retirement pension, but the amount available can vary enormously, as explained below.

Final earnings schemes

The 'final earnings' pension (the commonest type for larger employers) is based on your years of membership of the scheme, your pensionable earnings at the time the pension is calculated, and the 'accrual rate', which means the rate at which your pension builds up. Typically, someone leaving at 65 with 40 years' service gets $\frac{40}{60}$ or $\frac{40}{80}$ of their pensionable earnings as a pension. You can usually convert part of the pension into a tax-free lump sum. In the Civil Service and other public services, you get the lump sum automatically, without having to give up any part of your pension. The starting pension is lower than it would be in a good private sector scheme ($\frac{1}{80}$ of final earnings for each year of service, rather than $\frac{1}{60}$), but it is then guaranteed to rise in line with inflation.

If you retire early, your pension calculation can suffer in three different ways:

▸ You will have had fewer years in the job, so the pension will be calculated on shorter service.

▸ Your earnings on which the pension is based are likely to be lower than you might have expected if you had stayed in the job.

▸ You are going to be drawing it for much longer. If the employer wants to keep the amount spent on your pension the same as if you had worked to the normal retirement age, there has to be an 'actuarial reduction' in the pension income paid so that the same pot of money is spread over longer.

A full actuarial reduction could mean that somebody taking early retirement at 50 sees a cut in the pension, after the reduced years of service have been taken into account, of 70 per cent.

There are also some complications relating to DSS rules. These arise because most schemes are contracted out of the State Earnings-Related Pension Scheme (SERPS). The scheme then guarantees to provide the equivalent of what you would have had from SERPS, at the same age as it would have been paid by the State (60 for a woman; 65 for a man). This guaranteed amount is called the **Guaranteed Minimum Pension** or **GMP**. In order to safeguard this commitment without spending extra money on it, some schemes will not allow you to draw an early retirement pension at all, or they restrict the lump sum that you can take.

How much pension schemes offer In practice, most pension schemes do rather better than the DSS minimum. They often have different scales of benefit, depending on the reasons why you are leaving. The least generous pensions are usually paid when you take early retirement because you wish to, rather than because of your health or at the suggestion of the employer.

A recent survey showed that more than half of the pension schemes covered gave a pension based on all potential years of service up to normal retirement age where someone was retiring owing to serious ill-health (so, for instance, a 55-year-old received ten years' credit to take service up to 65). There might be a lower level of benefit for those who are less seriously ill, based on accrued service and partial credits. Alternatively, there may be a permanent health insurance (PHI) scheme, giving a proportion of earnings for as long as you are sick.

For redundancy, the same survey found that about half the organisations covered gave a pension which was calculated on the basis of service done, but then 'actuarially reduced' to take account of the early payment. A typical reduction would be, say, 3 per cent for each year not worked; a 55-year-old would then lose 30 per cent of the pension by retiring ten years early. Around 10–15 per cent of organisations in the survey provided a pension based on actual service but not reduced for early payment, and the rest either gave some credits or gave an unreduced pension for those over a certain age and a reduced one for younger people.

Getting the best possible deal However, the details in scheme booklets may tell only part of the story. Often there are unpublished rules, or the Personnel Department may have authorisation to go over the normal limits in some cases. So it is always worth negotiating to see whether there could be more to come. If a whole workplace, or a whole company, is being closed down, there is likely to be much less scope for this than if selected people are being asked to go. Again, there is usually a difference between large and small companies here. The larger ones, with a public relations image to think of, are likely to be much more generous than the smaller ones.

Frequently a trade-off is offered between the (non-statutory) redundancy lump sum and the pension.

Alternatively, you may be able to use part of the redundancy payment to buy extra benefits. This can have tax advantages and also give you more income to live on. Check that you know exactly what is on offer and how it works out. Ask for an interview with your Pensions Department if you are at all unclear. Think about the following:

▸ What lump sum are you being offered, and how much pension must you give up to buy it? Because you would expect to draw the pension for longer, a younger person should be offered a higher lump sum per pound of pension given up than someone of 65. So check if this is so in your case and, if not, ask why.

▸ How long will the pension and lump sum take to come through? There can be a nasty gap between the last pay cheque and the first pension cheque. It's easy enough to arrange an overdraft or to take money out of your lump sum, but it could be difficult if it catches you unawares.

▸ Have the trustees given more in practice in the past (and so might be expected to do so again in the future)?

▸ What pension increases are being made under the scheme rules? In the public sector, no increases are given until you reach the age of 55, but then a 'catching up' increase raising the pension in line with the rise in prices (not earnings) is given. This is much less common in the private sector.

▸ What is payable if you die before starting to draw the benefit?

If the pension on offer is quite small, or heavily reduced because of early payment, it might be possible to defer it and draw it later. However, any special increases may be on a 'take it or leave it' basis, so that you lose them if you defer. You may also find that if your health subsequently deteriorates, you cannot then start drawing the deferred pension but have to wait until the scheme's normal retirement age.

Money-purchase schemes

The other sort of pension scheme – the type more often available in small companies – is a 'money-purchase' scheme. In this type of scheme, your money and any contributions from the employer are invested (usually with an insurance company). When you retire you can take a certain amount as a lump sum and the rest of the fund is used to buy an annuity, which provides you with a pension for the rest of your life.

Depending on the terms of the contract, you may find that you lose out heavily by retiring early with a pension of this sort. There are several reasons for this:

▸ Less money will have gone into the scheme, and it will have been invested for fewer years, so the amount available in the scheme will be less than if you had carried on until normal retirement age.

▸ Each pound's worth of annuity purchased will cost more, because you can expect to draw it for longer.

▸ Many insurance contracts apply heavy penalties if a contract is terminated early.

It is generally not possible to renegotiate one of these contracts at the time when the early retirement or redundancy arises. The only way to get a better deal, therefore, is for the employer to put in extra cash to fill the gap. How easy this is will depend on the reasons for the job loss.

Other payments

You may have a number of other payments to come in your final wages – such as 'weeks in hand' (money held back by your employer from your wages when you originally started work), holiday payments, payments for time off in lieu that you have not taken, or accumulated bonuses. There could also be money due from a share-save or share option scheme.

Check out what you are entitled to, and try to get any disputes settled before you leave, when they will be easier to deal with. If you run into problems, talk to your union or staff association, ACAS, or the local Citizens Advice Bureau.

The company car and other non-wage benefits

You may be offered the opportunity to

▸ buy your company car;

▸ continue subscriptions to BUPA or other organisations at a preferential rate;

▶ continue being covered for life or disability insurance at your own expense but without needing a medical examination.

It is *usually* worth taking up these offers, if they are things you can make use of and you will be able to afford any other running costs. On the other hand, if the company car is a large high-performance one, and you are planning to move to the countryside and run a craft workshop, you might not want to take it. But you might be able to come to an arrangement to swap it for something more suitable; it is always worth asking. If your health is dubious, then insurance benefits without a medical examination could result in a substantial saving. Check (with an accountant, or the tax office itself) what the tax position would be.

Mortgages and other subsidised loans

In some sectors, such as financial services, employers are offered subsidised mortgages and other low-interest loans. Those who leave lose these, but they may be phased out over several years. National Westminster, for instance, ends the mortgage subsidy two years after the employee leaves (even if the person is being made redundant). At Barclays there is a seven-year wind-down period, during which the rate is increased gradually each year until it reaches the customer rate.

You may have to pay for a life insurance policy to cover the mortgage, if this has been included free in the past.

You may be able to negotiate special terms at the time you leave, or you might want to use some or all of your lump sum to reduce the debt.

Membership of associations

Your workplace may have an occupational pensioners' association. Large numbers of these have sprung up in recent years; they can help with networking and offer social events.

Cable and Wireless has an active association which acts as the first port of call for any complaints, runs a regular magazine, and has dinners every so often in different areas of the country.

They may also have access to 'welfare funds' or similar pots of cash for people who are experiencing hardship. Because of the number of people who have taken early retirement in many firms, occupational pensioners' associations these days are often dominated by 'young' pensioners in their 50s.

You may be offered continued membership of your union, staff association or professional organisation. Often there are reduced membership rates for retirees, or special branches. It would often be worth taking this up, at least for the first year or so until you are set in your new direction.

Enforcing your legal rights

As we have seen, good employers usually offer a package that is considerably better than the statutory minimum. If this is included in your contract of employment, or in a collective agreement covering you, or if it has become 'custom and practice' over a period of time, this should be legally enforceable. But even the best employers usually retain a certain amount of discretion, or make sure that there is some small print in the rules to allow them room for manoeuvre if the costs become higher than they expect – so you will need to check the relevant documents before taking the matter further.

If the employer, or someone in a position to speak for the employer such as the local Personnel Manager, makes a firm commitment relating to the package you will receive on redundancy or retirement, they may well have created a contract which they are bound by – even if it turns out that they have miscalculated the figures. If they press you to take action as a result of an estimated offer and you then do so, again they could have created a binding commitment on their part. You will be in a much stronger position to argue this if you have something in writing – whether from yourself or from them – than if you are relying simply on your understanding of a conversation.

In a 1995 report, the Occupational Pensions Advisory Service (OPAS) had some firm words to say about the number of complaints they had received concerning incorrect early retirement quotations. They pointed out:

'administrators sometimes seek to avoid the consequences of this mis-information by hiding behind the fact that when the quotation was given it was described as being an estimate . . .

'Our view is that the word "estimate" cannot be used to excuse a mistake which results in figures significantly lower than those first given . . . the Pensions Ombudsman shares this view.'

So it will always be worth contacting OPAS or the Pensions Ombudsman (see 'Useful addresses') in such cases.

Personal pensions

Some people will have their own personal pensions, rather than being in an employer's scheme. You will usually be able to draw a personal pension from the age of 50 onwards, but it will probably be heavily reduced, especially if you haven't been paying into it for very long. Ask for an estimate, and think about whether you can afford to continue it even for a few years longer, so that it has time to accrue a greater return on investments. In many cases you will be able to suspend contributions (though there could be a charge for doing so), so you can start paying into it again when you are earning. You won't, however, be able to pay any contribution towards a personal pension in any tax year in which you have no earnings at all. So if you are planning to stop paid work altogether, check what will happen and take advice on the best way to deal with it.

For full information about personal and occupational pensions, see *The Pensions Handbook*, published annually by ACE Books.

The tax position

The tax position relating to payments at the end of your job varies.

Lump sums

Certain lump-sum payments made on redundancy or severance are not taxed in full. The first £30,000 of such payments is exempt, and only the excess is taxed. Examples of such payments are:

▶ genuine *ex gratia* payments on termination of employment; this means payments that are not included in the contract of employment and do not form part of the wider terms and conditions of employment, including established practices (they are treated as pay in full if they are included);

▶ statutory redundancy payments and lump-sum payments for loss of employment from the employer's own non-statutory redundancy scheme;

▶ payments made because the employer has been in breach of contract, for instance by not giving the notice required under the contract, and compensation for wrongful or unfair dismissal.

Where as part of a package the employer provides something which is not a cash payment, for example the use of a company car for a period of time, the value of this provision has to be determined and added to the cash amount. The total amount is then taken into account for the purpose of deciding what is taxable.

Your employer ought him/herself to check the details and ensure that you do not pay more tax than you need. If there seems to be no sign that this is happening, suggest that the firm approach their accountant, or ask for information at an Inland Revenue Tax Enquiry Centre (listed in the phone book).

Lump sums payable from the pension scheme, as part of a retirement or early retirement package, are tax-free (with a very few exceptions; your Pensions Manager or Personnel Manager will tell you if any of these apply to you).

Pension payments

Pension payments are always taxable, normally under PAYE. An employer paying out a pension will deduct PAYE at source just as if it was earnings, as will an insurance company or any other provider. In general payments from permanent health insurance schemes set up by the employer (see pp 126–127) will be taxable, but if you have set up your own policy it will not be. Check the position with your local tax office.

Certain social security benefits such as Incapacity Benefit (except for the short-term lower rate) or Widow's Benefit are also taxable. The value of the benefit and the employer's or personal pension are added together in order to work out your tax coding, and then all the tax is deducted from the pension.

If you are receiving earnings as well as a pension, you will need to be sure that the employer and the pension scheme are aware of each other's existence, so that the tax coding can be adjusted. If you are self-employed, include the pension on your tax return so that it can be taken into account. Contact your local Inland Revenue Tax Enquiry Centre (address in phone book) if you are not sure what to do.

How social security benefits are affected
Redundancy and severance payments

If you have left without serving out the full notice period (whatever the reason), then part of any 'compensation' from your employer for the termination of your employment is assumed to be in lieu of any notice that you should have been given. This would apply, for instance, to a severance payment. So you are not entitled to Unemployment Benefit (or Jobseeker's Allowance after October 1996) for any day which would have been covered by that notice and can be treated as covered by that compensation. This is called the 'ineligible period'.

For this purpose, 'compensation' is defined as any payment made when you leave, which would not have been made if you had not left, except:

▶ pay for the period before your employment ended (such as weeks in hand, or a bonus for work already done);

▶ holiday pay;

▶ a statutory redundancy payment;

▶ a refund of contributions to an occupational pension scheme.

The 'ineligible period' always begins the day after your employment ended. If part of your payment was in lieu of notice, then the 'due date' when the ineligible period expires is the day when any notice which you were entitled to (by statute or in your contract), or would have been entitled to if you had not waived it, would have expired. (See pp 16–17 for details of notice entitlements.) If you had a fixed-term contract, the date when the contract was due to expire is the due date. The maximum ineligible period is a year.

As explained on page 17, if you are made redundant at the same time as at least nine other employees, your employers have to consult any recognised trade union at least 30 days before making the redundancy (or 90 days if 100 or more people are affected). If the employer says that part or all of the redundancy payment is in lieu of these rights, then the ineligible period ends *either* when the consultation period would have ended *or* on the 'due date' explained above *or* on a 'standard date', whichever is later. The standard date is calculated in weeks by dividing the amount of the payment by 206 and rounding the answer down to the nearest whole number.

If the employer does not say whether any part of your lump-sum payment is compensation for lack of the statutory notice, then the ineligible period is treated as ending on the standard date.

Before you leave get a statement in writing of how the payment has been worked out, and take it to your union or the Citizens Advice Bureau if you are unsure what effect it will have on your benefit. You have a legal right to such a statement under Section 102 of the Employment Protection (Consolidation) Act 1978.

Pension payments

The amount of your pension lump sum is not taken into account when calculating the 'ineligible period' explained above, so make sure that it is clearly separated out in any statement you receive. But the amount of pension that you receive does affect your Unemployment Benefit (Jobseeker's Allowance after October 1996). Until October 1996, for anyone over 55, if the pension is more than £35 a week, Unemployment Benefit will be reduced pound for pound above that level. After October 1996, the threshold figure for non-means-tested JSA (see pp 116–118) will be £50 a week, but the rule will apply at any age. This applies to both occupational and personal pensions.

NOTE The amount of any lump-sum and pension payment will have a direct effect on your entitlement to means-tested social security benefits, such as Income Support, the means-tested element of JSA or Housing Benefit. These are covered briefly in Chapter 10, but for more details see *Your Rights*, published annually by ACE Books, or the Child Poverty Action Group's *Rights Guide*.

Checklist on ending your job

Notice period

statutory

under contract of employment

any payment due in lieu of notice?

Consultation period

any payment due for waiver?

Redundancy payments

statutory

employer's scheme

will any of it be taxable?

expected tax deduction

Pension scheme – available on early retirement as

pension

lump sum

deferred sum

what annual increases are payable?

Other payments due at end of employment

bonus

holiday money

weeks in hand

share scheme

Preferential terms on other company assets

car

BUPA or equivalent

subscriptions to union, staff association or professional organisation

life assurance

other

Total lump sum expected (after tax)

£ _____

Total pension (after tax)

£ _____

Has the offer been confirmed in writing?

Do you have a breakdown of the figures?

When will it be payable?

Is the package structured in the most tax advantageous way?

Effect on claiming UB/JSA: what will be the 'ineligible period'?

CHAPTER THREE

What do you want to do now?

As pointed out in the Introduction, losing your job can be an opportunity for a new start rather than a threat. The fact that you have done one thing for many years is no reason for assuming that all you can do is more of the same. If you want a change – or if you have to make a change because there are no opportunities left in your old occupation – then go for it. Decide what change will suit you best and work out what you have to do to achieve it. This might be a new full-time job, or some mixture of part-time work, consultancies and voluntary work.

The first step is to carry out an audit of your current position. Think about:

▶ what money you will need, or want, to live on (both in the immediate future and in the years ahead, when you finally do retire);

▶ what skills, aptitudes and knowledge you have which would be of interest to an employer or useful to you in self-employment;

▶ what you like, and are interested in, and feel you are good at.

You also need to think about the limits on what you can do, such as:

▶ your health;

▶ your family commitments (to children or elderly relatives who might need care in the near future);

▶ where you live – whether you can travel and what your feelings would be about moving house.

This chapter takes you through this audit step by step.

Your finances

If you are single, or the sole earner in the family, then the answers to the questions in this section will be based on your whole family unit. If, on the other hand, you have been a dual-earner couple so far (or your partner is in a similar position to you and seeking new employment), then to start with decide whether you are working out everything on a shared basis or looking at each person's needs and income independently. Although you may manage your finances separately, in practice people who live together are almost always *interdependent* financially, so it usually makes sense to work it out on a shared basis.

How much money do you need?

Basic living expenses

It is important first to define what is meant by 'need'. First of all, there are the inescapable commitments of yourself and your partner and family, such as:

▶ mortgage or rent;
▶ Council Tax;
▶ food and other basic necessities;
▶ HP and similar payments;
▶ heating bills and transport.

You may also have commitments to other people – putting a student son or daughter through university, for instance, or paying maintenance to an ex-spouse.

Tot up the cost of these essentials at their current level (that is, not taking account of any inflation). If you have a computer, put all these figures on to a spreadsheet; it will make it much easier to play around with the calculations later.

Leisure activities and extras

But when you pare your finances down to that level, it's difficult to enjoy life. Enjoying life tends to cost money, and some hobbies and interests cost a lot more than others. Some people feel that life is not worth living unless they can go on an expensive ski-ing holiday each year, while others prefer a quiet walk in the country.

If you have not done this sort of calculation before, working out the cost of your leisure activities can be quite a shock. But there is no need to feel guilty or ashamed about this, or to feel that you have an obligation to cut back your expectations of life. You may have to if your plans do not work out as you had hoped. In the short term you may want to be rather frugal until you see how things work out. But no one should feel that they have to pitch their sights too low.

Providing for your retirement

Think also about your needs when you retire and have to live on whatever pension you may have. It is difficult even to guess how much you will need in 15 or 20 years' time in money terms, because of the effects of inflation. However, it is possible to estimate what you need to put into a pension scheme as contributions to get a decent amount.

If you find employment that includes a pension scheme, you could expect to pay an average of about 5 per cent of your earnings as an employee's contribution. If you are on your own, and having to buy a pension out of your own resources, then you need to think of putting away *at least* 15 per cent of your net earnings each year.

In both cases, if the pension you have built up already is not very good, or non-existent, you will need to put in a lot more if you are to build up enough for a comfortable retirement over a short period. Only if you have already got a very good pension, and you are sure that it is going to keep up with inflation, can you say that you do not need to worry about any further provision for your retirement.

Your total income requirement

By adding a pension contribution figure to the amount you have calculated you need for a comfortable lifestyle, you will have got a net figure for your income needs. To find the gross figure (which is what you see in job advertisements or what would be quoted to you in an interview), you need to add back tax and National Insurance. Working this out is complicated, because of the need to take account of your personal allowances (the amount of income you are allowed to receive before you become liable to pay Income Tax) and the part of your earnings on which you pay

National Insurance and tax at lower rates. Roughly speaking, if you are looking for a lower-paid job you will need to add about another 20 per cent; you will need around another 30 per cent if you will be paying basic-rate tax. If your expectations are higher and you would be paying tax at the 40 per cent tax rate if you achieved them, it is more complicated. You would be paying 40 per cent tax on part of your income only, and above a certain level your National Insurance contributions will not rise any more. So add perhaps 37 per cent to the take-home pay figure you have worked out (unless you feel like doing it more exactly).

Jack and Mary have decided they could just about manage on an income of £12,000 a year after tax. Grossing that up by adding 30 per cent brings them to £15,600. However, a comfortable income of £20,000 a year would mean £26,000 after grossing up.

What income will you have?

On the other side of the equation comes your income. If you have started drawing a pension from your employer, that can go into the balance sheet on that side (at its gross, pre-tax figure since you have already worked out a gross needs figure).

If you have a reasonable lump sum from your pension scheme or a severance payment, think about how much of it you will want to invest and what income you could receive. (Alternatively, you might want to use some of it to reduce your outgoings, by paying off mortgage or HP debts for instance.) Be conservative in your estimate of investment returns, because you will not want to take big risks or to start eating into your capital. At present (October 1995), a return of 5 or 6 per cent would be reasonable on a low-risk investment.

If you have no pension yet, either because you were too young to draw one or because the terms offered were too bad for it to be worthwhile taking it now, all or most of your income needs will have to be met by earnings.

Think, too, about whether any shortfall is long-term or short-term. If you are due to get a reasonable pension and a lump sum in four or five years' time, your attitude to the income you want now may be different from that of someone who has not yet built up much of a pension.

Jack and Mary will have Jack's early retirement pension of £7,000 from his firm. They will have £50,000 altogether in savings after they have spent part of Jack's severance payment on a trip to Australia. So they can look for investment income of £3,000 a year, at a 6 per cent rate of return, giving them a total pre-tax income of £10,000. So the gap between their currently expected income and their 'comfortable' budget is £16,000 a year. The gap between their income and the 'just about managing' budget is £5,600.

If Jack and Mary are going to manage at all, they have to earn *some* other income. But even to reach their 'comfortable' budget neither of them needs a 'proper' job like Jack's previous professional management job, which was more than full-time and really took over his life. A limited amount of consultancy work, full-time work at a less taxing level, or reasonably well-paid part-time jobs would do. And they need to do rather less if they are happy to move to the 'just about managing' lifestyle – in effect, buying extra leisure through reduced working time.

What are you worth?

In parallel to looking at your financial position, consider what you might be worth to an employer or to those who might buy your services. You know what you *were* worth until very recently, because you were being paid a wage or salary by an employer until you lost your job.

If the reason you lost your job was nothing to do with you or your skills and abilities, it is a reasonable starting assumption that you are worth just as much now. You might, for instance, have worked for a company that went into liquidation, but in an industry that is still thriving. Or you might have been with a foreign parent company that took a strategic decision to withdraw from the UK.

On the other hand, the circumstances of your job loss could have an effect on what you are worth (without in any way reflecting on you as a person) in the sort of role you had previously. If you are a middle manager whose employer has been 'downsizing' or 'delayering', you will know that there are a lot of other middle managers in that position and that there will be a glut on the market. If you are highly skilled but in an industry that has largely disappeared, such as shipbuilding, those specific skills will have lost their market value. You will need to invest in adapting them to other markets, or obtaining new skills, before you can put a market value on your job again.

Whatever you do, don't assume that you are too old to learn. 'You can't teach an old dog new tricks' is just a myth. Research projects have shown time and again that, to quote one report from the then Institute of Personnel Management (now the Institute of Personnel and Development):

'although older people do not learn as quickly as their younger colleagues, they can in fact acquire substantial new knowledge and skills . . . Older people can be particularly effective learners after their anxiety in learning situations has been overcome and opportunities for practice have been provided. Further, older workers do not forget new knowledge and skills any faster than their younger colleagues.'

Although going through the job ads is not a particularly good way of finding a job as an older person (as explained on pp 46–47), it is well worth keeping an eye on them to see what is paid for jobs that compare with yours. It is extremely important not to underprice yourself, because if you do so others will undervalue you too. (Even if you don't need the money and are planning to offer your services as a volunteer, it is worth knowing the value of what you are giving.) One adviser says:

'I've had people assume that they are bound to have to take a cut in pay, which is not always the case. They may take a lot of convincing that the work they have been doing for our firm has given them skills which are readily transferable elsewhere.'

She cites the example of one woman, with considerable financial skills, who assumed she would need to look for a job earning around £20,000 and ended up with one paying £100,000.

What have you got to offer?
What skills and abilities do you have?

As the example above shows, the fact that one employer has taken you off their books does not mean that another one will not find your skills and abilities highly useful.

If you have been doing a job for a long time, and have perhaps developed it as you went along, it is easy to take what you do for granted. You may think 'there's nothing to it', simply because for you, there isn't – it comes as second nature after so long. You may also feel that your skill is in something very specific, when in fact it can quite easily be used elsewhere. Computing is a good example of this. Perhaps you have always worked with one particular accounting package, and feel that is all you know. But there are strong similarities between different accounting packages; with some practice and a short period of training, you could be just as proficient in many others. It would certainly take you far less time to pick it up than someone starting from scratch.

Your skills and abilities may have developed *outside* work. You might be the backbone of the Parent-Teacher Association, treasurer of half a dozen groups, or champion cook for all the church fêtes and socials. Many people who are in dull jobs where they are unable to exercise their talents compensate for this by leading a far more interesting life in their own time. Are there skills which you could make use of – and would enjoy doing so – in a paid capacity?

A skills audit

To assess all this you need a skills audit. An alternative term for skills, very much in vogue, is 'competencies'. All this really means is what you are competent at. You can do this by yourself, but it's often better to find someone else to help you. To quote the authors of *Finding the Right Job*, the BBC book on the subject, 'It's surprising what they will include that, through false modesty, you will have missed.' Possible sources of help include:

The Careers Service Many people think that this is open only to youngsters, but in fact many local authorities provide adult guidance also. This is not a statutory requirement, though, so it may have fallen by the wayside in your area as a result of public spending cuts. Or you may need to pay for a consultation, unless you are on a very low income.

A commercial careers or employment consultancy You will find them listed in the phone book under 'Careers Advice' and 'Employment Agencies and Consultants' or see the 'Useful publications' section for a directory. Avoid wasting money (and your own time) by checking out first exactly what they can offer, and preferably getting recommendations from someone else. One of your first questions, a recent *Guardian* article suggested, should be whether they have other clients like yourself. The cost, if you have to pay yourself, could start at £1,000 for 'individual counselling and a general CV and career brush-up'. Try to persuade your employer that it is worth referring you and your colleagues to one of the firms that works only on this basis, and also paying the fees.

The local Training Enterprise Council (TEC) (or Local Enterprise Council – LEC – in Scotland) As part of the service they provide to the Government for unemployed people, they will do a one-hour interview and aptitude test for people referred to them by Jobcentres. Self-referral is also possible. Alternatively, they may contact the Careers Service to do this for them.

All these organisations have different approaches, and some allow much more time for thought than others. At Coutts Career Consultants, for instance, they suggest that clients should virtually write a life history in a 'workbook' setting out what they have done. They expect the clients to spend a week or more over it. A TEC interview would be much quicker, and concentrate more on fitting square pegs into square (or possibly round) holes. But it would probably be helpful to do the exercise anyway, at your own pace.

You might like to enlist a supportive colleague, friend or partner (with the emphasis on the *supportive*; some people do thrive on putting down their nearest and dearest).

The BBC book quoted above suggests taking a large sheet of paper and ruling it in columns. In the left-hand column, list:

▶ Current job

▶ Previous jobs

▶ Family responsibilities

▶ Activities you do in your own time

▶ Formal education

▶ Training

Then at the top of the other columns put down the following headings:

▶ What I actually do or did

▶ The responsibilities involved

▶ Competencies this demonstrates

▶ My achievements

According to Brian Cooper of Coutts,

'People often find it very difficult to put down their achievements, because they were just "part of the job". I had one ex-sales manager who had succeeded in replacing a major competitor's products with his own in a whole new area of the market, but it took a lot of discussion to get this out of him.'

So make sure you blow your trumpet from the beginning – you'll need to at any interview.

What do you like doing, and feel you're good at?

These two factors do generally go together; it is easier to get to be good at the things we enjoy doing than the things we find dull (if only because we practise more). It is also difficult to like things we feel a fool doing. For example, some people enjoy selling – whether it's themselves as people, products or ideas. Others cringe at the thought. The first group are far more likely to be successful as sales representatives – no matter what they are selling – than the second.

Most occupations include some aspects that people like and some that they don't. One complaint that many people have when they reach a certain level is that they don't spend enough time doing *real* work, and they spend too much time doing paperwork and in meetings. In the public sector and large private firms, there has also been a tendency for everyone to have to do more form-filling, as appraisal, performance measurement and checking of standards take hold. Many teachers, for example, feel ground down by the demands of the National Curriculum and Standard Assessment Tests.

There could be aspects that would make a potentially dull job interesting for you, or that would make a potentially good one unappealing. Being a receptionist in a lively office, with lots of people coming and going and a lot of phone calls, might suit a gregarious person perfectly. The same job in a different office might mean being shut away in a small room with piles of routine work to get on with.

You are almost bound to have to take on some activities you don't enjoy – but you want them to be outweighed by things you do enjoy doing. You are perfectly entitled to take all these things into account in your search for new work. The fact that you have been pushed into the search, against your will or with mixed feelings, does not mean that you must take 'whatever there is'. You have a right to a choice.

The need for money, and the requirements of the 'Jobseeker's Agreement' (explained on pp 117–118) may, however, mean that you have to take something that is not what you want. If you find that you have to take a job at a level you don't want, treat it as an experience and a learning opportunity. Carry on your search for work you do want, in an organised way, as described in the next chapter.

The more you can play up your strengths, the more likely you are to succeed in your search. Your feelings about particular subjects are going to come over to potential employers and customers. 'Infectious enthusiasm' does really exist. If you are bubbling over with anticipation and ideas about what can be done, you will come over as positive and a good bet. If, on the other hand, you put yourself forward for something you know you will hate, because 'it's a job', you will probably come over as negative and downcast – so why should an employer pick you out from anyone else?

So now add three new columns to your large sheet of paper, headed 'Likes/dislikes', 'Important to me' and 'Good at/bad at'. Add another section in the left-hand column, called perhaps 'The future' or 'Potential work'. In filling these new columns in, think of less tangible things as well as more concrete factors. These columns could include:

▶ as a liking, a secure pay cheque at the end of each week or month;

▶ as something you dislike and are likely to be bad at dealing with, financial uncertainty and insecurity;

▶ as being important to you, working with a congenial group of people;

▶ as something you are good at, relating to people and helping with their problems.

Again a careers adviser, consultant or friend may be able to help you with this by talking it through. You might be offered psychometric tests, which aim to measure your interests and aptitudes through the way you respond to certain questions and tasks. These can be helpful, though many people are cynical about them. They can be dangerous if misused. Make sure anyone offering them is accredited to do so. They should be either a chartered occupational psychologist or qualified under the British Psychological Society's scheme. Tests that look at your personality, rather than simply your aptitudes, should *not* be done unless there is sufficient time for a proper follow-up discussion. In any case, they are only *guidance*, not gospel. One of the skills they show is simply how good you are at taking tests.

Your limits

Whatever you may want to do, and however adaptable you may feel you are, there will still be some limits that you want, or feel it is necessary, to impose. If you do not have your own car, for example, you will need to work somewhere accessible by public transport from your home. If you have caring responsibilities, perhaps for a parent or an in-law, then you may not be able to move away from your present home even if the perfect job comes up elsewhere. If your health and fitness are not brilliant, you might need a job that is indoors and fairly sedentary. Any of these factors, and others, could limit the hours you can work (both the length of time, and when the hours are worked). Shiftwork and unsocial hours, for instance, are difficult for many people, but there are others whom they suit. Someone with a family and plenty of social life might not want to work weekends or evenings; a single person without much going on in their life might even prefer to work those times.

Consider how much time and money you will need to spend travelling. A journey that takes, say, an hour each way will be a waste of a good chunk of your life if you do only a three-hour session when you get there. It might be better to plan to work two or three full days in the week, to cut down on the journey time and the fares.

Your thoughts on all this go into the 'Future' or 'Potential work' section of your worksheet (or, if you prefer, on a separate sheet). Don't make too many assumptions about being unable to change your habits, or your family being unable to change theirs. No one is ever too old to change if they want to.

What would you like to do?

You now have a detailed picture of your financial position, what you can do, what skills and knowledge you have, what you like doing, and what limits you want to set yourself. So now try and turn all that into something more concrete in terms of what you are looking for, where, and for how long. The sample checklist on pages 44–45 sets out some points to think about, but you may prefer to put together your own. The last section is intended to give you space to write a specification for the sort of role you really want, but you could extend this considerably.

If you have several different interests, you might feel several different roles would be acceptable – either as alternatives or doing a bit of each.

A variable plan

In life, of course, nothing goes according to plan. So you may well find that you change your mind as time goes on, or that you can't find just what you want and have to compromise.

You may be able to foresee changes in your financial position that mean you want to do different things as time goes on. Perhaps you are currently too young to draw a worthwhile pension from the firm, but you know that in five or ten years' time you will have X amount. So you might want full-time work only for the next five years (though there would be no need to tell an employer this), followed by a period of part-time work and then by full retirement.

Alternatively, you might want to work full-time or nearly full-time but not want – or feel you could get – one task that would give you this. So you might be looking for several part-time jobs. Such a 'portfolio' of jobs may well involve a mixture of employment and self-employment, but the end result – in terms of what it feels like and the demands it makes on you – are likely to be much closer to the self-employed end of the spectrum. Many people thrive on the variety and meeting a lot of different people.

So if you are planning to change your pattern of work over the years, or to take on a portfolio of tasks, adapt your own specification to match.

Hours

Tick one of the following, or put in order of preference:

under 10 hours a week ☐   between 10 and 20 hours ☐
between 20 and 30 hours ☐   full-time ☐

Working pattern

Tick one of the following, or put in order of preference:

regular 9–5 type hours ☐   regular but not necessarily 9–5 ☐
happy with irregular working pattern ☐

Place

Tick one of the following, or put in order of preference:

very close to home ☐   within half an hour's travelling distance ☐
within an hour's travelling distance ☐ prepared to move house or live away from
             home if necessary ☐

Working

Tick one of the following:

for someone else ☐   as my own boss ☐
in a partnership ☐   employing other people ☐

Weekly or monthly figure needed: £

Field of work

Tick one of the following:

same as my previous occupation ☐ development from it ☐
something different ☐

If you've ticked 'development' or 'something different' write down on the next line what you have in mind.

Training and education needed

Tick one of these:

not necessary at this stage ☐ recognition of skills or competence
updating of current skills   I already have ☐
or competence ☐   training to develop new skills ☐

Sort of work

Tick one or more of the following, but try not to contradict yourself!

routine ☐

developmental ☐

stimulating ☐

needing use of
imagination ☐

office-based ☐

management role ☐

caring tasks ☐

using craft skills ☐

using new technology ☐

manual labour ☐

indoors/out of doors ☐

sitting down ☐

involving travel ☐

physically strenuous ☐

not strenuous ☐

working under close
supervision ☐

using own initiative ☐

other (add)

Now write your specification of the work you want:

The next step

Armed with this specification and your plans, you are ready to start your search, whether it is for a job, a business to set up in, training or education opportunities, or voluntary work. The next few chapters cover the different factors that arise in each case, and how to set about the search for what you want.

CHAPTER FOUR

Working for an employer

This chapter looks at the different types of paid work that are available, such as

▶ full-time

▶ part-time

▶ job shares

▶ temporary/casual

Before looking at any of this, however, this is the best place to tackle the problem that has probably been worrying many readers.

Age discrimination and how to combat it

However hard you try, will the new job ever be there, at your age? Many people feel that, for those in their 40s and 50s, searching for jobs is a meaningless ritual because older people are so discriminated against. That there *is* discrimination cannot be doubted. Richard Worsley's book *Age and Employment* (see 'Publications from ACE Books'), which aims to encourage employers to think again about older workers, discusses the evidence and the way discrimination operates.

The most obvious example of age discrimination is in job adverts in newspapers and magazines. Time and again these specify age limits, though there is no obvious reason why a 46-year-old accountant, for instance, should be any worse at doing the job than a 43-year-old. This does limit the field in which you can look; on the other hand, the majority of jobs are *not* filled by advertisement. Instead, they are filled via speculative approaches or contacts – people being asked if they are interested, or hearing about the job and expressing an interest. Low-paid, manual or routine clerical jobs, and part-time jobs, are often filled in the traditional way by people calling in at the firm after the Vacancies board has gone up, or through cards in newsagents' windows. With higher-paid and higher-status jobs it tends to happen more elegantly, through 'networking' – getting to know the right people and persuading them that you are worth considering for a vacancy.

The professional organisation dealing with personnel and human resources management, the Institute of Personnel and Development, takes a strong line against age discrimination. Its policy statement says that it 'believes that the use of age criteria in employment decision making is unfairly discriminatory and harmful to both individuals and organisations'.

Its *Statement on Age and Employment* extends this with detailed arguments and recommendations. If you come across a particularly blatant example of discrimination, it could be worth drawing the employer's attention to the *Statement*, or writing to the Institute about what has happened.

As an individual older person faced with employers' prejudices, it is the initial step – getting an interview – that is probably the most difficult. So you need to make the maximum use of all the informal contacts you have, and also to make speculative applications wherever suitable. One outplacement adviser said, in discussing this:

'It's ironic that when we are looking at discrimination against women or ethnic minorities, we are insisting all the time on fair advertising and interview procedures. When we are counselling older people about finding new jobs, it's the other way round, we are telling them how to get past the barriers in the system by taking all the informal routes.'

In any contacts with employers, you must stress what skills and competence you have, what *you* can bring to the job. It is not wise to leave your age out of a CV altogether (see p 59) but it can come well down the list, *after* you have explained all the things you can do.

Encouragingly, there are some signs that employers are now taking a more reasonable view about older workers. Eileen Ridley, at Wallsend

Jobclub, reports that a survey they did recently showed that many employers *favoured* older workers because they regarded them as more reliable than younger ones.

The outplacement adviser quoted above felt that, at least in London, older people with some skills and training who genuinely want jobs will succeed in getting them. Some of those that don't succeed, she thinks, are rather 'going through the motions' because they don't want to admit that really all they want is a good rest. Outside London, and for people whose skills are not in short supply, it is rather different. The problem lies in the general jobs market, and the high level of unemployment, exacerbated by age discrimination – not, it must be stressed, by any personal qualities you gain or lose as you get older!

Full-time work

Full-time jobs are probably the most difficult jobs to find, simply because everyone wants them and the number available is shrinking rather than growing. Only a third of the jobs created since the winter of 1994 have been full-time.

You may be looking for work at the same level as before or at a less taxing level; in the same sort of occupation or in a different one. Those looking for work fairly like their previous job may well get considerable help from outplacement services and employment consultancies. People looking for something different may have to do rather more for themselves. But you are still likely to have a network of contacts you can use, if the area you want to move into is something you have developed outside work.

Consider looking for temporary work, perhaps as a holiday relief, or casual employment in your chosen field. Often, employers wanting to fill a permanent job will look first at those they know already and can trust. They can even create, or bring forward, a job for someone who has already shown that they fit in with the organisation. Ray Lowrie, who runs the Jobclub dealing with the highly skilled workers of the defunct shipbuilders Swan Hunter, was reported in a newspaper article recently as warning Jobclub members 'that it is unrealistic to expect to find a permanent job immediately; they must see short-term work as a means of proving themselves'.

Part-time work

Part-time work tends to be easier to find than full-time, but it is a lot more variable in terms of what is offered and how well paid it is. It tends to be worse paid than a full-time job doing much the same thing. Part-timers can also find themselves treated as 'non-people' when it comes to discussions of policy, opportunities for training and promotion, and so on. But part-timers now have exactly the same employment rights as full-timers, whatever their hours (see p 16). According to European law, discrimination against part-time workers may be considered to be indirect discrimination between men and women (since the vast majority of part-timers are women). It is then only allowable if it can be 'objectively justified'.

Though part-time work is spreading to almost every sector, it is particularly common in areas where there are marked peaks and troughs of work, or where the job needs covering for longer than a working day. Examples are retail shops, catering and hotels, banking and other financial services, and caring jobs in residential homes and hospitals. There are also possibilities where there is a specialist job to be done but it does not warrant a full-timer – a part-time accountant or bookkeeper might be needed for a small business, for instance.

You might find that your own previous employer, or a similar one, would be able to afford to employ you part-time though they could not afford to have you full-time. For instance, owing to public spending cuts, many schools are having to replace full-time staff with part-timers. It may also be worth applying for jobs that are advertised as full-time, but where the employer may be happy to accept one or more part-timers, or to arrange a job-share (see below), if people with the right skills come along.

One trap that part-timers can fall into is ending up as cheap full-timers, doing extra work that they are not paid to do just because there is too much to fit into their part-time hours. People working for voluntary organisations, and in demanding jobs like social work or teaching, can find themselves caught up in this way. Get it clear with the employer, from the start, what your hours are going to be, and what work you are expected to do in those hours. Stress from the start that you have other commitments you intend to maintain.

Don't confuse *part-time* work with *temporary* work. There are many jobs which are both part-time and temporary, and some indeed shade over into casual work. But there are also permanent part-time jobs in which people can, and do, stay for many years.

Job-sharing

This is a particular form of part-time work where a full-time job is divided into two. The job is usually split down the middle, with half the wages and half the non-wage benefits for each person. One person can work mornings and the other afternoons, or one can work at the beginning of the week and the other at the end, or you can do alternate weeks. There may also be a session of 'overlap time' when you are both in the workplace in order to hand over tasks and bring each other up to date.

Although the costs might be slightly higher than employing a single person, the attraction for employers is that usually the job-sharers will arrange to cover for each other during sickness, holidays and other absences. Vacant 'halves' of an already established job-share are sometimes advertised, or two people can get together and apply for a job on a job-share basis. If the employer has not heard of the concept before, or has not tried it, they may take some convincing that it will work. New Ways to Work (see 'Useful addresses') can provide material explaining how it works.

Zero hours contracts

These again are a particular form of part-time work, very close to casual work. The idea is that you are offered no regular pattern of employment but are called in as and when you are needed by the employer. Some of these contracts virtually require you to sit by the phone all the time, waiting for the employer's call. They are popular with certain types of employer whose demands for labour are irregular and unpredictable but not, in general, with employees (for fairly obvious reasons). They also tend to pay pretty badly.

Check the terms of the contract and what your rights and responsibilities are. If the workplace has a union, join it to reduce the chances of being exploited.

Casual or sessional work

In some areas of work, such as the media, there are widespread opportunities for casual work and they are spreading still further. As with part-time work, your old employer or a similar one may be willing to employ you for odd sessions.

Ian used to be a senior cameraman at a TV company. He took early retirement, but is now working for them on a sessional basis, about one day a week.

Those with nursing qualifications may well be able to find work through a 'nurse bank', established by a local health service trust, and teachers may be able to work on supply with the local authority. There are also various specialist employment agencies now setting up in different sectors of education and further education.

If the work involves a lot of preparation – as lecturing or teaching may do, for instance – the hourly rate you are offered for the occasional session may not be worthwhile. But working in this way could give you a way in to more regular employment, and might also be a way of testing out whether you will really take to some new activity you are thinking about. If, for instance, you were thinking of running a pub, then doing casual or part-time work in your local pub would be a good way of seeing all sides of the operation.

Doing casual or sessional work can play havoc with your social life and other commitments. Nor will it suit a person who needs to know where they are and hates uncertainty. But if you can build up a relationship with one particular source of work, you should quite soon be able to predict when the calls will come and how much notice you will get. As a casual worker you will almost certainly be working some unsocial hours, because those will be just the times when the full-time regular workers are off and your services are needed.

In many casual jobs, the line between employment and self-employment is blurred. There can be tax problems if it is not clear which side of the line you fall on – see pages 78–79 for more details.

Teleworking

This means working for an employer, but based at home (or you may be treated as self-employed; see pp 78–79 for more on this).

Nearly three in ten firms now have employees who work from home, or are planning to start. This can be useful if you have caring responsibilities, or if you need to work (on telephone selling for instance) in evenings or at weekends but don't want to travel late at night. But especially if you are living alone, working like this can become very isolating, and you may come to feel almost a prisoner of the phone or the computer. Some firms offering teleworking also offer ways of getting people together now and then, so check if this is possible.

CHAPTER FIVE

Looking for a job

This chapter deals with the whole process of looking for a job. It covers:

▶ the initial research you need to do;

▶ how to go about looking for work, including approaching people 'on spec' when you don't know if they have a job going or not;

▶ developing job-hunting skills and putting together information about yourself (almost always known by the Latin term *curriculum vitae* or CV);

▶ preparing for an interview.

Doing your research

If you are thinking of changing your occupation – whether moving into a completely new field or into one that is a development from your previous job – it will pay to do some research before you go much further. Even if you plan to stay in the same field, but have been with the same employer for a long time and are not very familiar with changed conditions, this will be worthwhile. Possible sources of information about particular occupations will be:

The local Careers Service library (see p 38), which will have a wealth of information. They may be able to offer an interview to take it one stage further. A Jobcentre may similarly have some material.

The local bookshop or library A shop like Waterstone's or Dillons, or a local reference library, should have a shelf or two of material about careers. The publisher Kogan Page, for example, specialises in this area and has nearly 30 different titles available. You may feel that you have had one career and don't want another, but the books are full of useful information and addresses; the publishers stress that they are intended for 'anyone wanting to start anew'.

The professional or trade organisation concerned Many such organisations have useful leaflets or handbooks, and some may have a careers officer you can talk to.

Friends, colleagues, or contacts who are already in the field As well as being a possible source of work, they will be able to tell you the pros and cons, and the points to watch out for. So long as you don't make excessive demands, most people don't mind finding the time to chat about their job over a drink. There is a sort of mutual exchange principle at work here: perhaps someone else gave them a similar helping hand at some point, or perhaps they may need some help themselves later.

The earlier you lose your preconceptions, the better. According to one adviser, for example:

'A lot of people seem to have a vague idea that they'd like to "work for a charity", and that this would be an easy and unstressed role. But these days, nothing could be further from the truth. There's an organisation which runs courses about working for a charity (Working for a Charity; see 'Useful addresses') and I persuade them to go on one if I can.'

If as a result of doing some research you decide that your chosen area of work is not for you, don't despair. Go back and revise your life plan. You haven't wasted the time if it enables you to make another constructive move. In any case you are not likely to be successful in your search if it is clear that your heart isn't in it and you know that the employment you are pursuing is not for you.

How to start looking

There are three main ways to look for jobs, and they are all worth trying at once:

▶ answering advertisements;

▶ making speculative enquiries by letter and phone;

▶ by word of mouth or 'networking' through people you know.

In a few cases, once you make contact you may be told to turn up for an interview without more ado. Much more often, though, you will be told *either* to fill in an application form *or* to send in a CV with a covering letter. On the basis of these, the people doing the recruiting will draw up a shortlist and ask applicants to come in for interviews.

When you make enquiries about a job (from any source) you will usually be sent a **job description** explaining what the job is and what you would have to do. You may also get a **person specification** explaining what sort of person they are looking for, and the skills, training and personal qualities they must have. (When you actually get into the job, you may find that these are works of fiction rather than fact!) It is *essential* that you read these through carefully, along with any information you are sent, or can find, about the employer and the job, before going on to the next stage. The more you can demonstrate that you match the needs the employer has set out, the more likely you are to be shortlisted.

Advertisements

Job advertisements are the bread and butter of many national and local newspapers, and you should always study them. Your particular trade or profession probably has some specialist magazines that you can look at in the reference library. Many professional organisations also send out bulletins to their members. And then of course there are advertisements in Jobcentres, employment agencies and newsagents' shop windows.

When you see an advertisement that interests you, take down all the details or take a photocopy, and *do what you are told*. If it tells you to write or phone for an application form, it is a waste of time to send in a CV at this point; wait for the form. If it sets a closing date, make sure you stick to it. Keep a note of the advertisements you have answered and the progress you have made.

Speculative enquiries

Many employers do not bother to advertise jobs because they already have a pool of people waiting for an interview, both those who have applied previously and those who have written in to them. So it is always worth sending in a letter asking about opportunities in a firm. Phone first to find out the name and address of the person you should write to. Look in company directories and other reference material for details of firms in your locality that might have the right sort of job.

Speculative letters need to be short and to the point. They should be personalised rather than photocopies, which give the impression that they are just 'round robins'. Say that you are interested in working for that organisation, and explain what you are looking for and what your skills are. Enclose a copy of your CV (see pp 58–62). Ask for an appointment to visit the company, to discuss the chances of employment there. Enclose a stamped addressed envelope for their reply.

Some companies will not respond at all, some will send a curt acknowledgement, and others will say that they will keep your details on file until a vacancy comes up. Others, again, may invite you for an informal interview. Prepare for this just as you would for a formal interview (see pp 63–65).

If you do have an informal interview, send a thank-you letter afterwards, saying how keen you are to work within the organisation. If later you see an advertisement for a job with them, when you write in you can remind them of your previous contact.

Networking

This simply means making use of all your contacts to find out about openings and to get yourself interviewed when you might not otherwise be. Quite often, an employer will leave open a short-term vacancy (such as a maternity leave replacement) because it is too much trouble to go through a full advertising and interviewing process for the sake of a few months. Or they may be thinking about creating a new job but have not yet got round to it. But if the right person turns up, this may stimulate them to do something.

The people you approach may not be able to help you directly, but they may be able to offer you new leads about where to look and information you should have; they may also share experiences. It is not a one-way process and you are not 'begging' for help in any way. You will be reciprocating by giving them ideas about what's going on in the world outside their own jobs, and offering your own ideas and information. People will also know that they can network with you in the same way when they need to, and this is valuable: no one feels altogether secure in their jobs today.

Start by making a list of all the contacts – family, personal, social and work-related – that you have. Then systematically make contact with anyone who you think might be able to help. This could be just for a drink and a chat or for a more formal 'information meeting'. Prepare for this as you would for any other interview (see pp 63–65). Keep a note of what you are told, and follow up further leads. Look in *Finding the Right Job* (see 'Useful publications') for some more ideas on this.

Finding resources and developing job-hunting skills

An early task in the job search project is getting the right equipment for the job, however modest: paper, envelopes, stamps, and cardboard files so that you can sort everything properly without wasting time.

A second step is to identify the nearest sources for things like photo-copying and printing off good-looking letters and CVs. If you possess a computer but only a poor-quality dot-matrix printer, or none at all, it could be worth investing in one that produces good-quality print. If there is no one else around much of the time to take messages, or if they are unreliable, then think about investing in an answerphone as well.

Going to an outplacement agency or a Jobclub

If you are referred to an outplacement agency by your employer, they should help with all this. Alternatively, you may be able to get into a Job-club, run by the Department for Education and Employment (or for them, by external contractors). Places in these are made available immediately to those affected by a mass redundancy, those coming out of the forces, or people with a disability. Others are referred by Employment Service staff after six months' unemployment; there may be a waiting list to join. You are allowed to remain with them for a limited period – 13 weeks at the Jobclub in Hadrian House in Wallsend, for instance. Both Jobclubs and outplacement agencies can offer help with vital job-hunting skills, for example:

▶ how to draft a CV;

▶ how to fill in an application form;

▶ how to make a speculative enquiry by telephone and write a letter in response;

▶ how to do well at interviews (sometimes with the help of a video, which can be terrifying but worthwhile).

The following sections go into these various aspects.

Preparing your CV

CV stands for *curriculum vitae*, which is a Latin term meaning, essentially, the course of your life. It should be a brief document. As one book puts it: 'If it's longer than two sides of A4 the recruiter may not take the trouble to read through it.'

It has to be accurate and well thought out, because its aim is to present you to the employer as someone worth interviewing. Ideally, you should write a new one for each job you apply for, but this may not be practical if you are following up several leads each week and cannot easily churn out different versions on a computer. The alternative is to do one standardised one, and then send off photocopies as required with a personalised covering letter.

There are several good books on finding a job that go into the details of writing a CV and give examples. See the 'Useful publications' section for some of them, or go and look along the shelves in the local library or bookshop. They should enable you to put together a good one. If you don't feel confident about it, an employment consultancy, the Careers Service or a Jobclub can help. There are firms of consultants which will help you draft and produce a CV, for a fee. They are of very variable quality, however, so ask to see examples of their work before parting with your money.

All the guides stress the importance of keeping your CV clear and simple – and positive. Stress what your skills are, not what your formal job title was. Nurses, for example, have considerable knowledge of computers these days. But an employer faced with an application from a nurse for a job involving work on computer databases may not look twice at it, unless the relevant skills are highlighted; the employer may not know what nursing involves today.

At least two of the books available give lists of 'action words'. The first few in one list are 'accomplished, approved, assisted, authorised, budgeted'; they suggest sprinkling these liberally around your text. There are several different formats for a CV, but the information that always needs to be included is:

Name and personal details, such as address, phone number, age and marital status. Some people say you should leave out your age here, but recruiters tend to become suspicious about gaps, so it is probably better to put it in.

Skills, competencies and achievements Include any major successes, and refer not just to the various jobs you have done but also to voluntary work or activities at home which have helped you develop particular skills.

Employment details It is usual to start with the most recent job and work backwards. Say what the organisation was and what department you were in. If you had a career break, say so (recruiters hate unexplained gaps; the only explanation they will think of is that you must have been in prison). If you took on particular roles such as acting as secretary of a voluntary organisation while you were on your career break, say so. Make it sound positive, not just a period when you were doing nothing.

Education and training, from secondary school onwards, including any vocational training you have done, and short courses within or outside the firm.

Qualifications.

Voluntary work, interests, hobbies If you are looking for a job in which your main skills and experience will come from something you have done outside your previous jobs, then put this section before the employment details and explain why.

Additional information.

References See below.

Write it in draft first, read it through (preferably with someone else who will pick up the errors you miss), and then type or print up a neat version.

A sample CV is shown opposite.

When you see an advertisement, or hear about a job that you want, send a copy of your CV off with a **covering letter**, equally well produced.

References

You will want to include details of a couple of referees on your CV, and most application forms also ask for names. It is normal to give your last employer as a reference, but if there is a good reason not to (for instance, that they have gone into liquidation) give the name of someone else who knows your work and explain why. The other referee could be work-related, or someone who knows you socially or from your leisure interests.

Check with the individuals concerned that they are happy to give you a reference, and ask them if you could see what they are sending, to be sure it is accurate. (Some people don't like showing them, though.)

If you have parted on bad terms with the previous employer, you may suspect that they will give you a poor reference. Talk to your union or staff association, or your solicitor, about this if necessary; there may be action that you can take.

For certain jobs, you may need a financial or credit reference. Talk to your bank manager about this.

NAME	**Elaine Jones**
ADDRESS	5 Any Street, Anytown
AGE	53

SKILLS AND COMPETENCIES

I am an experienced administrator with knowledge of:

- *the management of a sizeable budget*
- *a wide variety of computer programs*
- *desktop publishing work*
- *organisation and management of a communications programme for a large organisation*

My recent work in Health Services administration has involved successfully creating and taking responsibility for the internal communications programme for a Trust with a budget of £x million.With an annual budget of £x, I accomplished the drafting, printing and distribution of posters, leaflets and newsletters for x staff, on time and within budget. As part of this, I acquired 'hands-on' skills in a number of word processing, database and desktop publishing computer programs. I also have project management skills, working with both internal departments and external contractors.

This work has been in addition to taking a key role in the day-to-day activities of the Central Administration Unit in which I was based. I have created and maintained a workflow system for the Unit to ensure that the paperwork is dealt with speedily and customers' demands are met rapidly and accurately.

EMPLOYMENT DETAILS

1989–1995	Senior Administrative Officer, Central Administration Unit, X Health Services Trust
1982–1989	Administrative Officer, Administration Unit, X Health Authority
1972–1982	Clerical Assistant, DHSS, promoted to Clerical Officer, 1978
1964–1972	Career break while bringing up 3 children. During this time I also studied French and German at evening classes, leading to success at A-level French and O-level German; acted as Secretary of the Pre-School Playgroups Association; organised the school Christmas bazaar for 3 years in succession
1957–1964	Office junior, followed by Office Assistant, Bloggs & Co, Anytown

EDUCATION AND TRAINING

1951–1957	St X School for Girls, Anytown
1992–1995	In-service training courses in Computer Technology (including specific software packages), Administration, Working with the Media, Project Management. (Have been accepted for Open University Business School management course commencing January 1996.)

QUALIFICATIONS

1959	Pitman Shorthand and Typing, Certificate of Proficiency
1967	O-level German, A-level French, Anytown Adult Education College
1978	ONC in Commerce

VOLUNTARY WORK, INTERESTS, HOBBIES

Outside my working time, I am involved with a number of voluntary organisations in the local community and have used my desktop publishing skills to produce newsletters and leaflets for, among others, the Anytown Townswomen's Guild, the Council for Voluntary Service and St X School.

ADDITIONAL INFORMATION

I hold a clean driving licence.

REFERENCES

(2 names)

The covering letter

This can be on a standard model, but adapted for each job. It is best to write or type a new covering letter each time, rather than send a photocopy.

This is your introduction to the person who is recruiting for the job. It is there to explain why you are sending in your CV to this particular person. So it needs to say:

▶ what position you are interested in (including any reference number and where you saw or heard about it);

▶ why you are suitable: highlight reasons that are explained further in the CV;

▶ a polite ending saying that you hope to hear from them soon.

Again, check the draft before finishing it off.

A sample covering letter.

Dear . . .

I am writing in response to your advertisement concerning the job of Publicity Officer for the National Association of X.

I enclose a CV for your information. From this, you will see that I have been running publicity programmes for a major NHS trust for the last few years, and have skills in communications, desktop publishing and project management. I believe that I am well suited to your requirements and look forward to hearing from you.

Yours sincerely

Filling in application forms

These are used commonly by employers who have large numbers of applications, so that being able to deal with information in standardised form is important. They are also used by those who are anxious to provide equal opportunities and to ensure that people are not advantaged unfairly by the quality of their own presentation of information about themselves.

Before you do anything else photocopy the form, and then read the job description and all the other material that has come with it. Then start drafting on to the photocopy, and only copy this on to the original when you are satisfied. Type the answers, unless you are specifically asked not to. Otherwise, write neatly in black ink. Put all the relevant information that you have already gathered from your CV on to the form, making sure you answer the specific questions they ask. If there is not enough room for your reply in any section, use an extra sheet rather than cramming things in too tight. Some application forms these days are very complicated, so check you understand what is being asked, and if necessary get some help.

Many employers today do not acknowledge forms, but simply say that if you haven't heard within X weeks, you can assume that you haven't been shortlisted. This may seem rather impolite but it is understandable given the numbers they have to deal with. It's permissible to ring up to check that the form has arrived, but if you do any more you risk being marked out as 'pestering'.

Preparing for the interview

You may well have done a lot of interviewing in your time and feel that you know all about it. But it looks very different from the other side of the table, and you will need some serious preparation. 'I've known people like accountants go to an interview without having looked at the accounts for the company they're seeing,' one adviser says. 'That seems to me an extraordinary lack of preparation, and must make one wonder about how serious they are.'

Always check out before you go:

Where the interview is, how you get there, and how long you will need. It's far better to arrive early than late and flurried. If something goes wrong and you have a problem, phone and explain – they may well be forgiving.

What the organisation does and how the department you are dealing with fits in. Send off for the annual report, look the company up in the reference library, ask if they have any brochures and reference material.

What you should wear It is not entirely true that interviewers make up their minds as a person walks into the room, but appearance certainly has a lot to do with it, so this does matter.

Prepare by thinking about what questions the interviewers are likely to ask, and what will provide a confident, knowledgeable response. Play to your strengths. What you have got that younger people haven't is *experience*, so make the most of it. Talk about the things you have done, the lessons you have learnt, and what you could bring to the new employer. Show yourself to be approachable and adaptable. Don't give in to the temptation to rubbish your old employer, even if you are feeling bitter. That goes down very badly with interviewers, because they are afraid you will do the same to them in due course.

You could be interviewed by one person, or by a panel of several people at once. You may be asked to do psychometric or aptitude tests, and you may find yourself plunged into a group interview (where several applicants are in the room at the same time). Or there may be more than one interview – perhaps on different days – with different people. Usually you are warned beforehand of all these points, but if you are told nothing, ring up and ask what form the interview will take. At a senior level, you might find yourself involved in an 'assessment centre', where you could spend two days or more doing different tests and doing role-play and other exercises.

There are also some techniques of 'stress interviewing' which can create a very unpleasant experience. Some interviewers, as David Greenwood puts it in *The Job Hunter's Handbook*, 'seem to feel that an interview is an intellectual point-scoring exercise'. Faced with this, he suggests that you keep calm, appear unruffled, and 'think long and hard about whether you want to work for someone as inadequate as that'. Look at his book for more information about the various techniques and for suggestions about other books to read.

You normally get your travelling expenses paid if you are interviewed, but you may have to ask. The only case in which you may not get them paid is if you are offered the job and then turn it down.

If you don't succeed at an interview

If you don't get offered the job, don't treat it as an aspersion on you personally: you simply did not fit with what they wanted. Treat it as a learning experience; 'debrief' yourself about what you did right and what you did wrong, and make a list of points to remember for next time. If the interviewer used a technique you had not come across before, make some notes about what to watch out for if you come across it again. If you are offered feedback after the interview, take the offer up.

CHAPTER SIX

Working for yourself

Many people have an itch to be self-employed, and cash from a reasonable redundancy or severance payment can offer a golden opportunity. There is quite a lot of help available, so long as you fit into one of the Government programmes. You can take on work on a small scale, doing a certain amount of consultancy or specific projects. Or you can set up a small business, which might perhaps grow in future.

There are more and more self-employed people around, and many commentators see it as the trend for the future. But the failure rate for those setting up in business on their own is uncomfortably high: 400,000 new businesses start up each year, but one in four ceases to trade within four years.

The type of business can vary enormously, from those where the sole asset is yourself and your brainpower or physical skills to those which require very considerable capital and are intended to grow into something sizeable. On pages 68–74 we consider some broad categories of self-employment. First, however, we look at the sort of person you need to be and the skills and resources you need.

What sort of person do you need to be?

To make a living in any sort of self-employment, you need some organisational skills and a certain amount of self-discipline. In a book written for a recent BBC series, *Start a Successful Business*, Rosemary Phipps suggested the following golden rules:

Adapt to the market As she says, 'It's all too easy to do what you want to do, or what you think the market needs, without ever checking to see whether you're right . . . Nothing ever exists in a vacuum and you need to position yourself, your business and your product/service in relation to what is already in the market.'

Create objectives You need clear personal objectives and a realistic sense of your own strengths and weaknesses, along with the will to adapt as conditions change. Decide before you start whether you want to employ others or work only for yourself, and how hard you want to work – though if the business takes off you may find yourself working substantially harder than you bargained for.

Have the right attitude 'Overwhelming optimism tempered with common sense (or rather, uncommon sense)' is Rosemary Phipps' prescription. Among other things, you need to be able to persevere, and also to check people out (even your friends), rather than naively trusting them. Most people are to be trusted – but some are not.

Be willing to do things you don't enjoy for the sake of the business. Very few people enjoy paperwork and chasing up overdue debts, but to survive, you have to do these things. Some people enjoy selling their services, but for many phone calls marketing themselves are agony. It is important, though, to do it, and you are most unlikely to be able to employ someone to do it for you at the start. If you feel you just cannot do it, then self-employment is not for you. According to one adviser, many people do very well in their first consultancy, but then fail to get a second slice of work 'because they just don't know how, or don't want to try, to market themselves'.

Don't let failure get you down A lot of things will not go right first time. You will have a good many false starts when people don't respond as you hope, or when suppliers, contractors and competitors seem to be putting obstacles in your way. It helps if you have someone you can moan to about these things, but also someone who can offer constructive suggestions. This is where business counselling, discussed on page 74, can help. If you are someone whose equilibrium is a bit fragile, and perhaps gets easily depressed, self-employment may not suit you.

Think at the start about the effect on your family and other relationships, especially if you are planning something that will require capital and you will be eating into savings, and perhaps also going into debt. It is not a decision that should be taken by just one person in the family – all of you should be involved. So it is crucial that you talk it through, in depth, before committing yourself.

What skills do you need?

To make a success of starting out on your own, you need two different sorts of skill or ability:

The skill to make the product (using the term in its broadest sense) that you are marketing. So it might be knowing how to make corn-dollies, or advising on the way corrosion affects the paintwork on ships.

Business skills – the ability to organise yourself and your finances, to deliver the work on time, and to go out and find new orders.

Different types of self-employment

No self-employed person is quite like any other. But there are certain broad groups into which people fall.

Skill-based work

Your skill might be the one you learnt and practised in your job, such as repairing cars, dressmaking or computer programming, or something you have developed away from work. If there is a market for it, almost any activity can be carried out on a self-employed rather than an employed basis these days. It is even possible to set up in business as a vicar! An early-retired clergyman in Walsall has set up in the private sector, publicising his availability to take funerals, weddings and other ceremonies with a leaflet delivered through letter boxes.

Often you will be able to work at home, or to use your home as a base. Many of those starting up in a small way don't employ anyone else. Often some other member of the family keeps the books and sends out the invoices. Frequently all the family members get involved in answering the phone and taking messages. Investment in an answer-phone and/or a mobile phone tends to be a good idea, if you are not to infuriate them (and your customers, if you have teenage children who are incapable of taking clear messages).

Some areas of employment are overcrowded and not very well paid, like window-cleaning and sandwich-selling. Others can pay very well for someone who is properly skilled, treats the customers well, and is *reliable*. We all have experience of builders and other tradespeople letting us down or doing a shoddy job. Someone who can be trusted not to do so can get premium rates, and people will be willing to wait for their services.

Consultancy

This is a very broad term, but it covers mainly people who are selling professional or technical skills and knowledge. Many people think of doing this, and they may well get their first piece of consultancy work from their old employer or from other professional and business con-tacts who know their work.

An important factor in success is keeping yourself up to date. People pay consultants for their accumulated knowledge, not just for the hours they spend on the job.

This means reading the journals, keeping up contacts with your col-leagues, attending conferences, and – in many scientific areas – carrying out 'hands-on' research, and all this takes time. One day a week's consul-tancy could mean spending another two days briefing yourself, and this would make it uneconomic. So doing only a few hours a week of consul-tancy work, even in the area that you already know from your job, will not be practicable for all that long. You need to go into consultancy wholeheartedly, or not at all.

Casual work for an employer

In some occupations and professions, there are jobs which are treated as self-employment by the firm but which are really little different from employment. Sales representatives for insurance companies and other firms are one example of this, and media jobs such as sub-editing, camera work and sound engineering are another. In some sectors it may not be possible to find work in any other way, but this type of self-employment can represent the worst of both worlds. You have the insecurity of someone setting up on their own – and particularly in sales work you may be paid entirely on a commission basis and so depend on the results of your own hard work. You may have to invest a considerable amount in equipment for yourself, or pay a monthly subscription for 'office services', before you earn a penny on your own account. But the actual work you do will be dictated by others.

Make sure you understand the terms of what is being offered before you take on this sort of work. With sales work in particular, think about your own personality if it is not the type of work you have been doing already.

Some teachers went to work for insurance companies after taking early retirement, often thinking that they could sell products to their ex-colleagues in the staff rooms. Some were very successful but others hated it, especially the 'close' when they had to persuade the prospective buyers to commit themselves.

See pages 78–79 for the definitions of employment and self-employment for tax purposes. If your work comes wholly or mainly from one source, the Inland Revenue may question your status at some point.

Setting up a cooperative

Legally you are likely to be employed rather than self-employed in this situation, but it is included here because it is more akin to setting up your own business than to joining someone else's. The basic idea of a workers' cooperative is that it is owned by those who work in it. There are a number around, including some which have resulted from employee buyouts of existing firms which have gone into liquidation, or of privatised companies in the public sector. According to Ann Bonner of Durham Cooperative Development Agency, 'There's a growing number of co-operatives in fields like community care, where personal contact between the customer and the worker is all-important.'

You can set up a cooperative with only seven people, though many grow larger than this. You will need some people with ordinary business skills if you are to succeed, and you will also need to develop skills in working cooperatively, planning and running meetings. Some parts of the country have specialised Cooperative Development Agencies, but in others these have closed down because of funding difficulties. There is a national organisation called the Industrial Common Ownership Movement (ICOM; see 'Useful addresses') which can point to sources of local assistance or help out itself.

Buying a franchise

There are a growing number of franchise opportunities available – you have probably come across some of the more widespread ones, like Prontaprint and some Body Shops, without even realising that they are franchises. To quote Rosemary Phipps: 'What you will be doing is taking on an idea that the franchisor has already tested commercially. You then pay for the right to use the business name and pay the franchisor a royalty fee based on your sales.'

The size of the initial investment, the level of royalty fee, and the scope for developing things yourself rather than sticking to a predetermined plan will vary from one franchisor to another. Check out all the details just as you would if you were buying a business from someone else (see pp 72–73). Most banks have someone who can advise you on franchising, and the British Franchise Association (see 'Useful addresses') will also be able to help.

Setting up a small business

These can be almost anything that involves a marketable idea. For many mature people looking for a new start, the natural inclination may be to look at things like pubs, restaurants and bed-and-breakfasts, which one might call 'I've always wanted to . . .' projects. Some of these provide a good and satisfying living for their owners, but many others fail because of insufficient research and/or capital. The key is to check out exactly what is going to be needed, and not to proceed unless you are satisfied that those requirements are going to be met. Think about:

Your own skills and abilities Can you manage the staff, deal with the accounts and produce the quality your customers are going to expect, day in and day out?

Your stamina Pub landlords and restaurateurs, in particular, work extremely long hours and may take very little time off. The job can be pretty stressful when things are not going well.

The capital required This can be substantial. If you have taken over premises that have already been in the same use, you will still want to refurbish them in your own style. Conversion is even more expensive. It can then take some time to build up trade, but all the time you will be paying staff and suppliers.

Talk to people who have experience in the field. You may be able to find a specific course to go on, and there are certainly books to read. Ask your local careers guidance providers, use their library, and go through a Training Access Point (TAP; see p 97) to see what is available.

Your dream idea is probably based on a favourite pub, restaurant or guest-house, so why not ask the proprietor to sit down with you for an hour and go through all the important issues. You could also ask if you could work behind the bar or in the kitchens for a while, maybe as a holiday relief, to see how it suits you. Make sure that you are given your share of the worst jobs; these are what you will be doing, as proprietor, when one of your staff doesn't turn up.

Buying someone else's business

If you are buying a business from someone else, it is crucial to do 'due diligence', which simply means checking everything. Make sure that the accounts add up, and that you have been told everything important. A pub that looks viable at a certain rent from the brewery, for instance, may be totally impossible as a going concern now that they have trebled the figure. Ask as many questions as you need, get the answers in writing, and don't be satisfied with evasive answers. Use professionals to help you: an accountant and a solicitor, and a surveyor if it involves property.

Kenneth Lysons, in the ACE Books publication *Earning Money in Retirement*, suggests the following checklist of points to find out about, both by asking the vendor directly and by researching in the library and the immediate area:

▶ When was the business established, and by whom?

▶ How many subsequent owners has it had, and why did they sell?

- What are the annual profits? Are these audited? Is the profit trend increasing or decreasing? What are the reasons?
- Are the premises freehold or leasehold? If leasehold, how long has the lease to run? Can it be renewed?
- What condition are the premises in? Will much renovation be required?
- Are equipment, fixtures and fittings in good condition? Who owns them?
- What is the condition of stocks? Are they new or obsolete, shop-soiled or deteriorated?
- Are suppliers dependable? Are any agreements due for renewal?
- What is the present and likely future competition?
- What is the location like?
- Why does the present owner wish to sell? Are the reasons given the true ones?
- What is the reputation of the business in the area? To what extent does this depend on the personality of the present owner?
- Are the present staff efficient and willing to stay on?
- How does the business compare with others that are available?

Get-rich-quick schemes, pyramid sales, etc

There are all sorts of schemes around promising you riches if you just undertake this course, or start producing or selling that product. Some are honest, but bring you income only up to the point where you have saturated a rather small market. Others are plain dishonest. There is only one good piece of advice so far as they are concerned, and that is Avoid Them. As David Greenwood says in *The Job Hunter's Handbook*:

'If you discovered a means of making a huge amount of money legally for very little effort what would you do? Would you share your secret with the world or would you sit back and quietly watch your bank balance grow? . . .

'Beware! Their effortless way of making money is probably through the stream of cheques and postal orders which they attract from gullible punters who respond to their advertisement.'

Or, to quote a cliché which must have been around for several centuries, 'If something seems too good to be true, it probably is.' Don't hand over money without asking someone independent to check the project out, and report it to the police if it looks dodgy.

Where to get help
Training

Training Enterprise Councils (TECs), or Local Enterprise Councils (LECs) in Scotland, can provide training or business skills through their **Business Link** projects, though it may be easier to obtain in some parts of the country than others. Business Link can provide training, advice and support to people setting out on their own. What it provides varies somewhat from area to area, so you will need to check what is available locally. Projects are currently being set up across the country; by mid-1995 about 50 per cent of those planned were in operation.

Business Link has high street offices – on Tyneside for instance there are four – where you can make an appointment. Staff will normally do a 'diagnostic' interview (this whole area is full of jargon) to discuss the various ideas you may have, and may also be able to arrange for you to have a specialist legal or financial interview. You may then get a place on a one-day information session and be allocated a **business counsellor**, who will have a continuing relationship with you over the next couple of years.

TEC/LEC courses are designed to help you develop a business plan (see p 76), and they also lead to an NVQ (see pp 94–95 for more details on these) in business management. The business skills course offered by Tyneside TEC has 12 modules. If you can show that you have already covered some of the work, the training provider can accredit you with that part of the qualification without expecting you to repeat it. Someone who was already qualified as an accountant would not need to go through the accounting modules, for instance.

Funding

There might also be start-up funding from your local TEC/LEC. The type of support, the eligibility criteria, and the 'brand name' (the name used in the publicity) vary greatly from area to area, so that sadly what is available to one person may not be there for another just because they live a few streets away.

To take the example of Tyneside, applications have to be accompanied by a business plan and an appraisal of the project from the business counsellor who is assigned to help you; they are considered at a panel meeting held once a month. You will qualify only if you are setting up a new business in which you intend to work full-time (36 hours a week or more), obtaining work from several sources. Technically you need to be unemployed when you apply for the money (though this can mean for just one day) or under notice of redundancy.

In the Tyneside case, the panel can accept or reject proposals; once rejected there is no appeal, no second bite at the cherry for the same idea – though you could go back with a different idea later. If you succeed, then you get a one-off lump-sum payment of £600, plus a series of progress review payments each quarter. These can be for meeting your 'action plans' or 'producing management accounts' or both. In total, over a period of 24 months, the payments come to £2,500. These are in addition to any profit you make, and so are taxable.

You can also get training vouchers which entitle you to the payment of all or part of the fees of courses approved by the TEC/LEC. These can be used up over a two-year period on suitable training from providers contracted to the TEC/LEC. Business Link counsellors will be expected to suggest what training you need, and you can then find out what is available from the TEC/LEC or a Training Access Point (see p 97).

There are many other sources of finance. Some of these can be contacted via Business Link, such as the banks. They may provide slightly better terms for someone who has been through the NVQ process. Other sources are local councils' economic development funds and specialist organisations like British Coal Enterprises, which can offer help to those who have worked in the coalmining industry, or will provide jobs for ex-coalmine workers. Business Link should have information and ideas about all of these. See also Rosemary Phipps' book for an explanation of the different types and sources of finance.

NOTE   There are also commercial firms that have set themselves up as 'grant-finders', charging a fee to give you information that is available freely from most TECs. Using one of these would generally be a waste of time and money.

Developing a business plan and management accounts

To receive almost any sort of assistance, you need a business plan. This plays the same sort of role, for someone starting up on their own, as a CV does for someone looking for a job. Work on the plan can take quite some time, as it involves:

▶ developing the details of your idea;

▶ doing market research, for instance by contacting potential customers to see if they are interested;

▶ investigating premises and staffing;

▶ working out budgets and cash-flow estimates;

▶ finding out what sources of finance are available and what offer the best prospects.

The time taken drawing up the plan will be well spent if it means that you have thought out how you will work and the issues involved. There are standard formats, and a business counsellor (from Business Link or another organisation that advises small businesses) or accountant will help you with them. There is also masses of literature on the subject (see the 'Useful publications' section).

Any competent adviser will insist that you are involved in drawing up the plan rather than leaving it to them; you have to 'own' it and be committed to what it says you will do, if it is to work. The plan is likely to need revision several times in the course of your first few months or years.

A business where the finances are at all complicated will need management accounts, so that you can tell if you are making a profit or loss and if there will be enough cash to pay the bills next month. Management accounts are best done as you go along; the courses and business counsellors discussed on page 74 will explain to you how to do these.

Tax, social security and VAT

If you are self-employed, you are responsible for your own tax and National Insurance. Tell the tax office and the Contributions Agency that you are in business to start with. Initially your tax office will be the one you dealt with when you were employed, though they may later transfer your file on. You can find the address of the Contributions Agency in the local phone book.

NI contributions

You will need to set up an arrangement for paying Class 2 National Insurance contributions. You can pay contributions every three months in arrears, or monthly by direct debit. These are paid at a flat rate and qualify you for most social security benefits, though not for Unemployment Benefit or the State Earnings-Related Pension (SERPS).

If you are just starting, your self-employed earnings may be low and you can apply for a 'certificate of exception'; fill in the form in DSS leaflet NI 27A. Apply as soon as possible, because this can be backdated for only 13 weeks. In 1996–97, you are entitled to this certificate if your estimated earnings are less than £3,260. If you have paid contributions for the year and it then turns out that you are below the limit, you can reclaim them by writing to the Contributions Agency (Class 2 Group, DSS, Longbenton, Newcastle Upon Tyne NE98 1YX) before the end of December that year. This does mean, though, that you will be creating gaps in your contribution record which could affect your pension later.

It is quite possible to be employed and self-employed at the same time in different jobs – perhaps working as a part-time assistant to someone for half the day and running your own business for the other half. You would then be taxed through PAYE on your income from employment and pay tax on a self-employed basis on the rest of your income.

If this is your situation, you can apply to postpone paying self-employed National Insurance contributions until after the end of the year, so that the employed contributions can be taken into account in working out what you should pay. Fill in and return the form in DSS leaflet NP 18.

Income Tax

You will also need to contact your local tax office. As a self-employed person you have to send in accounts and tax returns each year. On the basis of these, you pay Income Tax and Class 4 National Insurance contributions, collected at the same time. Class 4 contributions don't qualify you for any extra benefits, so really they are just another form of tax.

It is generally best, if your business involves much use of capital and any great amount of purchases and sales, to employ an accountant to sort out your annual accounts for the Inland Revenue. It costs money, but it is well worth it to prevent you paying more tax than you need. Even if you are only doing freelance work as an individual, you will find it useful to ensure that you have claimed everything you are entitled to as business expenses.

Employed or self-employed?

There can be problems about the definition of self-employment. The advantage, for you, of being self-employed is that you are able to offset the expenses of doing the work – such as buying equipment and supplies and travelling to see clients – against your income. You also save in National Insurance contributions (but get fewer benefits). The advantage for the employer is that they save on National Insurance contributions and do not have the same contractual commitments as to employees.

The Inland Revenue tend to conduct 'blitzes' in certain trades and professions, where they suspect that there is a level of phoney self-employment. They will then insist on treating people as employed, and requiring the employer to deduct PAYE and National Insurance from their earnings. This has happened recently, for instance, with many media workers such as sub-editors. The National Union of Journalists has taken test cases through the Inland Revenue's appeal system against this, and won. Some other professions have had to accept the Inland Revenue's ruling. Their views on the distinction between employment and self-employment are set out in leaflet IR 56/NI 39 *Employed or Self-Employed*.

If you answer 'yes' to any or all of these questions, they say, you are probably employed:

▶ Do you have to do all the work yourself, rather than hire someone else to do it for you?

▶ Can someone tell you at any time what to do, or when and how to do it?

▶ Are you paid by the hour, week or month? Do you get overtime pay?

- Do you work set hours, or a given number of hours a week or month?
- Do you work at the premises of the person you work for, or at a place or places he or she decides?

On the other hand, if you answer 'yes' to any or all of these questions, you would usually be considered self-employed:

- Do you have the final say in how the business is run?
- Are you risking your own money in the business?
- Are you responsible for meeting the losses as well as taking the profits?
- Do you provide the main items of equipment you need to do your job (not just small tools)?
- Are you free to hire other people on your own terms to do the work you have taken on? Do you pay them out of your own pocket?
- Do you have to correct unsatisfactory work in your own time and at your own expense?

There are some special rules for 'labour only subcontractors', who exist especially in the building trade. They receive a '715 certificate' authorising them to be treated as self-employed if they meet certain conditions.

Claiming social security benefits

While your business is developing, you may be entitled to social security benefits to help you survive. In particular, there is Family Credit if you have dependent children, or Disability Working Allowance if you have a disability which means that your earning capacity is limited. Both of these are means-tested benefits, which means that your income is made up to a certain level or an 'applicable amount' laid down by the Government. For self-employed people, earnings mean net profit, after various expenses have been met.

The DSS calculate your net profit by looking at your profit and loss account, and your trading account and balance sheet where appropriate. If you are only just starting, they can look at estimated figures based on a shorter period. They then work out a weekly figure by averaging your earnings over the period covered by the profit and loss account (or a different assessment period, if they are having to work on estimated figures). Complete weeks when you are not working, for instance if you are off sick or on holiday, are ignored.

VAT

VAT becomes payable once your turnover reaches a certain level. The rules are complicated and vary between types of activity. Ask for expert help to sort out what should and should not be VAT-able, once you reach that level.

Insurance

There are some types of insurance that businesses legally must have, and others that it is a sensible precaution to take out. This section summarises the position. See ACE Books' *The Insurance Handbook* for more detailed information.

Consult an insurance broker who has experience in organising insurance packages for small businesses. Most big insurance companies offer policies which package together the various types of insurance you need. The costs vary depending on the type of business and where it is based. Fire and theft insurance, for example, can be extremely expensive in some inner city areas.

Employer's liability insurance If you are employing someone outside your home, you are legally obliged to have this, to the value of at least £2 million, and to display the certificate on the premises.

Motor insurance If you have a car or other vehicle for your business, you must insure it just as with any other vehicle, but you may need to pay extra because you are using it for business purposes.

Public liability insurance The law does not require you to have this, but it is sensible to get it. This covers you against damages awards to members of the public who are injured on your premises or by your activities. (You will need this if you are trying to get a 715 certificate as a subcontractor.)

Product liability insurance covers you for damage caused by your products.

Professional indemnity insurance is useful (and in some professions compulsory) if your business involves the giving of advice. Many professional bodies bulk-buy insurance at a saving for their members. You may have had such insurance in your previous job, so check that the insurers will take your track record into account, rather than treating you as a new entrant to the profession.

Consequential loss insurance or **business interruption insurance** covers you while your business is out of action, for instance if the premises burn down.

Credit insurance covers you against the risk of your customers not paying up. You may not be able to obtain this until you have a track record in business, however.

Loan insurance

If you need capital to get your business started, this may involve borrowing money, remortgaging your house or personally guaranteeing a loan to the company. Go to reputable advisers to arrange this, and check that you fully understand the implications.

Consider taking out insurance to cover the loan in the event of your falling ill or some other disaster happening. This insurance is expensive, however, and you need to be careful of the small print. A recent report showed that in all too many cases the insurers managed to disclaim responsibility once a serious problem arose. So take expert advice before committing yourself and possibly wasting your money.

NOTE Before taking out any sort of loan, always check with your spouse or partner, who may otherwise find him/herself committed without realising it. The complications caused by this can be even worse if the marriage breaks up.

Pensions

Unless you are happy that the pension you are already entitled to from a past employer will see you through into a comfortable retirement, you will need to set money aside for a pension every year. The contributions you make towards a personal pension are tax-free, so they will reduce your tax bill, which eases the pain a little.

The older you are, the more you are allowed to put into a personal pension (30 per cent of your net relevant earnings between ages 51 and 55; 35 per cent between 56 and 60; 40 per cent if you are over 60). Unless you have already built up a substantial pension, you will *need* to put that sort of amount away.

The Pensions Handbook, published annually by ACE Books, gives details of what to look for and the pitfalls to avoid. Get independent financial advice, and check that the terms of the policy you buy are properly explained, and that they suit you.

CHAPTER SEVEN

Voluntary work

If you have a reasonable income, whether from a pension, investments or part-time work of one sort or another, you may want work which gets you out of the house, without wanting or needing to be paid for it. There are many opportunities for this, both with voluntary organisations and in public duties.

Searching for the right organisation

Voluntary work can be as rewarding or as unrewarding as a paid job, and for much the same reasons. Some organisations know how to use people properly; others simply waste people's potential and then wonder why the turnover of volunteers is so high.

If you find an organisation to work with and then find it doesn't work out well, you may be made to feel guilty about leaving them in the lurch. So it makes sense to take care in deciding what organisation to work for, just as you would with a paid job.

Start by making an audit of your position, as suggested in Chapter 3. Think about what you have to offer, and look at your skills and experience – again just as you would with a paid job. Think, too, about how much time you want to commit. According to REACH (see below), 'it's better to understate than overstate the time you want to give'.

Different types of voluntary work

Although it is a very broad generalisation, it would be fair to say that there are two alternative sorts of voluntary work open to you – or you might want to do both, at different times or for different organisations.

Making use of your skills

The first type involves using specialist skills and talents for the organisation. These might be the same as those you used in your job, or a development of them. Someone with management skills nurtured in a large organisation, for instance, might find themselves chairing a voluntary organisation's management committee.

You may already be involved with a group, and be able to take more on. Former bank managers, for instance, are likely to find themselves suddenly in demand to be treasurer of whatever groups they are involved in.

If you are a member of a particular profession or trade, you may be dragged into the administration of it – for instance acting as an examiner or tutor for student members, or sitting on one of the professional committees that usually burgeon.

Another possibility is to offer your services to a local charity or self-help group that seems to have the right sort of gap.

An alternative is to go through a bureau or agency. One national one is REACH (see 'Useful addresses'). The name stands for Retired Executives' Action Clearing House, but REACH deals with anyone who has a 'skill which can be transferred to meet charities' needs'. It finds part-time, voluntary jobs for retired or redundant people with business or professional skills who want to offer their expertise to hard-pressed voluntary organisations. Most people, they say, commit themselves for between one and three days a week, usually locally so that they do not need to travel. It can be for a fairly short, fixed period or it can be for longer, until either you or they run out of steam.

Some REACH volunteers take on a less demanding role than they had in their job (though, as already pointed out, work for a charity tends not to be a soft option these days), while others seize the chance to develop existing skills or learn new ones. There is no charge for REACH's services.

REACH operates from London, but it has recently appointed a number of regional coordinators who can visit volunteers. They ask you to fill in an application form giving details of your areas of interest (along with a CV if you want to send it); they then try to match this on their computer with the charities who have contacted them to ask for help, and send you a list. If you express interest in any of those put forward, REACH sends details to the charity so that it can contact you to discuss things.

John Cole formerly an engineer, was pictured in REACH's spring 1995 newsletter. He has become a regional coordinator for REMAP, an organisation which designs, makes and supplies technical equipment for disabled people where such aids are not commercially available.

You could find that your employer is willing to let you start a secondment with a voluntary organisation while you are still officially working for the firm. BT, for instance, has offered some people 60-day placements in community posts as a prelude to redundancy. As a press report on this pointed out:

'This gives people new items for their CVs; it makes them feel better about BT; it gives them an outside shot at finding a job in the organisation in which they are placed; and it gives them dignity at a time when they need it.'

Doing more general work

If you don't feel you want to use your particular skills any more, the alternative is to do 'general' work. This could be helping in a charity shop or sitting with people who have a disability while their carers have some time on their own. If what you want is the company and to give active support to the cause, this may be enough. To find work of this sort, you could

▶ ask in your local library if they have a list of voluntary organisations, and contact those you like the look of;

▶ contact your local Volunteer Bureau, if one exists (some have had to close because of spending cuts; contact the National Association of Volunteer Bureaux to see if there is one in your area – see 'Useful addresses');

▶ attend the Volunteer Fairs which are held in many areas during Volunteer Week in May each year. Organisations needing help set out their stall and try to attract people to offer their services;

▶ find out about opportunities during the local Age Resource week, run in May each year (see 'Useful addresses' section for details about Age Resource);

▶ go through the National Volunteering Helpline (0345 22 11 33) to find out what has been registered with them in your area.

You could, however, find that after a while, when you have recovered from the trauma of leaving your job, this sort of work is rather frustrating; you may well decide that you want more. One advantage of voluntary organisations is that they tend to be considerably more flexible than ordinary employers. If you want to expand your work or take on more responsibility, they will probably let you. If you have been open about what skills you have, the organisation may in any case be begging you to take on more. Voluntary organisations are remarkably good at pulling people into their net and persuading them to give more of their time and effort than they ever intended.

A prime example of an organisation that makes intensive use of volunteers, and also gives them a well-planned training and work structure, is the Citizens Advice Bureau (CAB). Originally CABs were almost entirely run by volunteers, but now most bureaux have at least a handful of paid staff. Much of the interviewing and follow-up work, though, and a large proportion of the administration, is done by volunteers; there are tens of thousands of volunteers involved in some 800 CABs in the UK. According to Libby Hinson, Deputy Manager of Gateshead CAB:

'Speaking for ourselves, we'd be extremely glad to see older volunteers. Many of those we have now are younger, and move on to a job or a course quite quickly, so that we have a constant turnover of vacancies. An older person can bring some stability and experience. Most of the problems we deal with are problems of everyday life. So someone who has had experience of life themselves, whether they have specialist knowledge or not, is suitable to be a volunteer.'

The essential skills, she says, are:

▶ being a good listener;

▶ being patient;

▶ being understanding without being critical;

▶ being non-judgemental towards people and their problems;

- keeping whatever you hear confidential;
- working as a member of a team.

Volunteers have to commit themselves for a minimum of six hours a week. The National Association of Citizens Advice Bureaux (NACAB; see 'Useful addresses') provides an eight-day training course spread over a number of weeks, plus self-study packs to help people to find their way through the information systems. There is a heavy concentration on interviewing and case recording skills. In some cases, such as Gateshead's, parts of the course are accredited through the national Open College network, so that they can be recognised elsewhere.

Many people carry on working for a day or two a week at a CAB for years, though there is generally an upper age limit of 70 for volunteers. The work can also act as a stepping stone to another job or to further education, as it rebuilds confidence and helps you develop and achieve recognition for skills. Once you have got through the training pro-gramme, Libby Hinson says, the most important factor – and this is true of many types of voluntary work – is reliability. You can be more flexible in your comings and goings than was possible in your paid job, but if you don't keep the managers informed so that they can plan a rota, you will be letting down the clients. 'Most clients don't know, and wouldn't care, that they are being interviewed by a volunteer,' she says. 'They've a right to just the same standards as if the interviewers were paid staff.'

Public service work

British society, especially at a local level, depends very heavily on the public spirit of retired and unemployed people. They sit as magistrates, as local councillors, and on all sorts of tribunals and committees. Some of these tasks involve a certain amount of payment, some of them no more than expenses.

Election to the local council

There are parish, district and county councils. In some areas of the country, it is possible to win a council seat as an independent. In most cases, though, you need to have been a member of your political party for quite a while before you get selected (though not necessarily a very active one; for 'unwinnable' seats they may be searching simply for candidates who will stand).

Tony started off by volunteering to start a Labour Party branch in his local village. But he was persuaded to show the flag by being nominated as a candidate for the local council, and won the seat in the general landslide of 1995. 'I need to get my letter box enlarged now,' he says ruefully.

Councils do not have nearly as much power as they used to. People are still a great deal more ready to give brickbats than bouquets, however, and you can find yourself dealing with a mountain of paperwork and long complex meetings. So being a councillor is not a task for someone who wants a little light work to keep them going.

Becoming a magistrate

Much of our system of criminal justice depends on the work of magistrates, local people who commit themselves to operate at the lowest tier of the court system. There are upper age limits for appointment (which vary in different parts of the country), but an early-retired person will often be able to meet them. The specialised Youth and Family Panel has lower age limits, however, and you need ten years' experience as a magistrate first, so you would be unlikely to be appointed to this.

In the busy Newcastle court system, for example, magistrates are organised in rotas; the aim is that they should sit for three days every four weeks. According to Betty, a former health visitor who became a magistrate after taking early retirement:

'You know well in advance what your days are, and you can plan round them. If you say you're available to do extra sessions at short notice they will probably call you in to do just that, so you have to harden your heart and say you cannot, on occasions.'

Betty was offered six initial evening training sessions, spread over a number of weeks. During this time she and her fellow trainees sat in on various court sessions, and also went on visits to the sort of places they might be sending people to, such as the local prison. After six months' experience on the bench, there were six more evening training sessions to complete the initial training. Every year there are optional refresher courses and specialist training for experienced magistrates.

Magistrates are not required to be experts in the law; they have clerks to advise them. Their role is to exercise cool judgement and common sense, after listening carefully to both sides of the argument. 'The most important quality', Betty says, 'is probably not to be too easily swayed. You have to weigh up how far you think people are telling the truth, and hold to your view if you think it is right, even if others oppose you.'

Sitting on a tribunal

In addition to the court system, there is a sizeable network of tribunals distributing 'administrative justice'. Some of these require particular knowledge of an area of the law, so that those sitting on them will tend to come out of a specific profession. Disability Appeal Tribunals, for instance, must by law include a member who is 'experienced in dealing with the needs of disabled persons . . . in a professional or voluntary capacity . . . or because they are themselves disabled'.

Others look for people with a more general knowledge of the area, or of living and working conditions, to assist a specialist legal chair. Social Security Appeal Tribunals (SSATs) or industrial tribunals, for instance, draw their members from a panel of individuals put forward in their area. The selection processes vary between the different types of tribunal; it will usually be best to ring the relevant central or regional offices and find out.

There is usually some training. For SSATs, for instance, there are a couple of daytime courses each year and some evening meetings. You are supplied with the main books, and kept up to date with a newsletter and journals at regular intervals. SSAT members are expected to sit about once every six weeks, though you can do more if you want and there are often requests to sit at short notice.

Other quangos and public bodies

There is also an enormous – and growing – range of other non-elected public bodies, many of which dispense large amounts of public money. These bodies range from health trusts to school governing bodies, TEC boards, Community Health Councils and many others. Some of the jobs, especially those chairing such bodies, are well paid but also demand a high level of commitment. Others may involve only monthly or quarterly meetings – though there is usually a pile of paperwork to get through as well. They may pay a flat fee for each day's sitting, or nothing at all.

Check that you know what the terms of reference are, including your liability if things go wrong. Decide also whether you support the policy that the quango has been set up to promote. The health service trusts, for instance, are there as part of the internal market arrangements for the National Health Service. If you do not agree with the general thrust of policy, you could find yourself a lone voice on the committee and rather unhappy. Check whether you will have some allies.

You can apply to have your name included in the list held by the Public Appointments Unit in the Cabinet Office (see 'Useful addresses'). This has over 5,000 names of people considered well qualified for public service, with a reserve list of a further 2,000. However, a recent newspaper report suggested that this is not the way in which most people get appointed to quangos: out of 2,481 appointments to quangos in 1994, only 143 were of people who had originally been identified by the Unit. It seems to be rather more a matter of networking and 'who you know'.

The effect on your finances

In most cases, voluntary work is just that, though you may get your direct expenses paid, some help in kind such as lunches, and an 'honorarium' to cover indirect and unquantified expenses. Public bodies may pay rather more; district and county councillors, for example, get their expenses and an attendance allowance for each meeting they attend.

Straightforward expense payments are not taxable, but other allowances may be. They *might* also affect your social security benefits. Check before starting any sort of voluntary or public service work.

Unemployment Benefit/Jobseeker's Allowance

As explained on pages 115–118, you need to meet some pretty rigorous conditions as the price of receiving Unemployment Benefit (Jobseeker's Allowance from October 1996). However, volunteers are allowed 48 hours in which to rearrange their duties in order to take up an available job. To qualify under this rule, you must be working for a charity or other not-for-profit organisation and not receiving payments other than expenses.

If you are receiving other payments, you will be treated as a part-time or casual worker. This could mean that your benefit is cut or stopped altogether for weeks in which you do the work. Explain the position both to the Jobcentre and to the staff of the voluntary organisation or public service body you are dealing with, and get their advice on what needs to be declared and in what way.

Incapacity Benefit

The rules for Incapacity Benefit require you to be unable to perform certain work-related functions, as explained on pages 118–121. If you have a clear-cut disability which scores sufficient points in the tariff system now being adopted – such as being in a wheelchair, or being almost entirely deaf – you would be able to do voluntary work without losing benefit. If, however, your case is more marginal, so that it is a matter of interpretation and the opinion of the medical authorities whether you are eligible for Incapacity Benefit or not, the simple fact of doing voluntary work, even for a few hours a week, could be used to show that you are not incapacitated for work. A light task at which you could be sitting down most of the time would probably be treated very differently from, say, conservation work restoring Hadrian's Wall.

Ask for advice from your doctor *and* from someone who understands the social security system (such as a local welfare rights officer) before committing yourself.

Means-tested benefits

If you get expenses for volunteering, which are no more than the amount you actually spend, they should not affect Income Support or other means-tested benefits. Other payments will generally be taken into account in full. Again, ask for advice if you are unsure of the situation. Most voluntary organisations will have checked on the position for their own volunteers.

Occupational pension or other payments from the employer

Voluntary work should have no effect on these. The only circumstance in which it could do so is if you have taken an ill-health pension which can be reduced or suspended if you recover. Doing voluntary work of the more strenuous type might then be considered to be evidence that you no longer qualify. Check the small print for your own pension scheme.

CHAPTER EIGHT

Retraining and education opportunities

If you have been in a job for much of your adult life, or looking after a family, you may not have had much formal training or education since the year you left school or college. You could have developed all sorts of skills 'on the job' and through in-company training courses, but have little to show for it in terms of letters after your name or bits of paper.

Other reasons for studying could be that:

▶ You have considerable qualifications but are unsure about whether they are up to date and still of value in today's labour market.

▶ You need some specific new training for a new project you have in mind.

▶ You realise that you are lacking in some very basic skills that you will need to help get another job. (You can be perfectly intelligent, and have held down a good job for some time, and still have trouble with spelling and arithmetic.)

▶ You simply feel that you want to learn something to keep your brain stimulated, or to develop a hobby or interest you have always had.

As stressed on page 37, no one is ever too old to learn.

Recognition of existing knowledge or development of new skills?

If you did the skills audit suggested on page 38 – and especially if you had some expert help with it – you will probably have identified areas where you need new skills, or recognition of those you already have. There are probably far more ways of obtaining these than when you were last looking for education. But the money available to finance courses is more limited, and you have to know who and what to ask.

Recognition of existing skills

Many people have been carrying out specific tasks in their employment for many years, without having sought or obtained any sort of certificate to say that they have done so. You might, for instance, have gradually taken on all the bookkeeping, or developed very substantial expertise in the welfare benefits system, but never tried to gain a qualification. Perhaps you were too busy, or it didn't seem necessary, or there wasn't an immediately suitable one. Or you might have a degree or A-levels in subjects completely different from those you are dealing with now.

You can obtain recognition for what you already know in a number of different ways. One possibility, for anyone who has been working in a particular discipline for years but has never bothered to gain a professional qualification, might be to put yourself through a crash course in it and take the exam at the end. Many of these qualifications are designed for people who are studying after work and in the evenings; they include correspondence material and some tutorials. It is worth finding out how quickly you could undertake what would normally be a slow process, and what the costs and demands would be. You could link in with courses run by a local college or another training provider. This might work, for instance, with someone who has been acting as an accountant or book-keeper at a higher level than their formal qualifications would show.

Or you could take an A-level in a suitable subject, perhaps a language you are already good at.

National Vocational Qualifications (NVQs) are the new form of practical training qualifications, replacing or running alongside older forms such as RSA, City and Guilds and BTecs. (Many of these in fact now work as dual qualifications, so you get something which is recognised under more than one body's rules.)

In general, you achieve an NVQ through a workplace; the employer works with an assessment centre to accredit you when you have reached a certain level of competence. There is no exam as such. But it is also possible to achieve one via a college instead, by means of work experience gained there and assessment by the tutor. Newcastle College, for instance, has created 'realistic' work environments such as typing pools and restaurants for people to gain their experience in. According to Sheila March, Course Adviser at Newcastle College:

'It may also be possible to achieve an NVQ, or part of one, through putting together a portfolio of work after you have left a job. There might be a time limit of, say, six months after you left the job, and you'd probably need the cooperation of the ex-employer so that you could collect evidence from your job. Some tutors would be very helpful.'

Another possible route is **Accreditation of Prior Learning**, a system that is only just getting off the ground. The idea is that you put together a portfolio of past work experience (not just in your last job) that shows that you've already reached the level of competence required to achieve an NVQ certificate. In Tyneside TEC's area, for instance, several colleges have developed pilot projects to allow people to gain access to different qualifications in this way. One college has done this with childcare, another with mechanical engineering.

Developing new skills

An alternative (or additional) possibility is to achieve new skills, or to bring those you already have to a higher level. If you have decided to change direction completely, you may need to achieve a qualification before you can start your new career. There are numerous courses available (see below on how to find out more about them). They might be provided by:

▶ universities;

▶ colleges of further education;

▶ the Open University;

▶ specialist institutes;

- ▶ training providers recognised by the TEC;
- ▶ other private commercial providers.

There are a great many mature students on courses at all levels, from the most basic numeracy and literacy courses to further and higher education; most institutions are keen to recruit them. There are a number of 'Return to Learning' and 'taster' courses for people who have not been in education for a long time, to help them find out what they can do and the best way to organise their lives around study. A good college will also give support and counselling to students, especially if they seem to be floundering. Open University courses, and others provided on a distance learning basis, are perhaps less geared to picking up such problems, but for those with some confidence in their learning skills they may fulfil just the right needs.

It is possible to start a degree course without any previous formal qualifications by doing a foundation year, either at the institution where you do the degree or at another one. Many courses are 'modular' now, which means that you may be able to join them at any point and pick up the bits you miss later. There are generally also 'transfer credits', which means that you can go elsewhere and have the work you have already done accepted, without needing to repeat it.

Finding out what's available

There are several ways to find out what's available and what might suit you. They are not mutually exclusive so you could try them all.

Training for Work

This is the adult training programme run on behalf of the Department for Education and Employment (DFEE) by Training and Enterprise Councils (TECs) and in Scotland by Local Enterprise Councils (LECs).

You will find that in different areas TECs and LECs have given different brand names to their adult training programmes. On Tyneside, for instance, it is known as Tyneskill Prospects.

You can be referred for training to a TEC/LEC-approved training organisation from several sources, including Jobcentres, Job Plan Workshops and Guidance Networks, or you can reply to direct advertising in the local press.

Guidance counsellors at these training organisations will help you assess your existing skills and talents and help you identify what training needs you have if you wish to pursue a particular occupation. They will have directories covering a full range of training opportunities that are available from approved providers.

The training opportunities that are available in a particular geographical area depend on the 'needs of the local labour market' (that is, what skills local employers say they are – or will be – looking for in the current and future job market). The level of the opportunities available under this initiative vary, and will range from fairly basic skills training through to training at management level. All training that you receive will lead to a National Vocational Qualification (NVQ).

It is up to the training providers whether they accept you on a course or not, and that will partly depend on whether they can get funding, and whether you fit into the 'profiles' they have developed with the TEC for their typical students over the year. Funding arrangements also depend heavily on 'outcomes'. So if the provider thinks that your chances of success are limited, they may not want you on the course.

If you are turned down, there will usually be somewhere else in the area where you can try again, but there is no formal right of appeal.

Training Access Points (TAPs)

TAPs are available at most career guidance or assessment centres, and in some other places also. They are computerised databases telling you what courses are available and where, and what each course covers. Usually there is a guidance worker to talk to as well, who will be able to take you through your options and help you find out more details. Look under 'Careers' in the local phone directory or ask at the local reference library to find out where there are TAPs in your area.

The education institutions

All further education colleges today are required to provide impartial advice and guidance on entry. Most will have a full-time worker to do this, with extra staff seconded to help out during the busy enrolment periods in the autumn. They should be able to guide you around and find the best course for you. Sheila March, at Newcastle College, might spend an hour or more with potential students (though usually it is less than that). She will go through what skills and knowledge they already have, and the reasons why they want to study something else. Most universities will have one or more people doing a similar job.

If you are looking for a part-time course dealing with an academic or leisure-linked subject rather than a vocational one, your local university's Centre for Continuing Education (which may have a different name locally), the Adult Education Service or the Workers' Educational Association will have some provision; the main reference library in your nearest large town should have details. The Open University can be contacted by phone, or they have a network of regional centres where you can visit and discuss your requirements.

Finding the resources

As usual, this is the difficult bit. How can you find the money to pay for a course which may cost several thousand pounds, and your living expenses as well? Resources are more limited today than they used to be, and students are expected to dig in their own pockets more and more. However, there are still sources of money available if you fit in with the various sets of rules.

Training for Work courses

Courses under the Training for Work system are free to people who are unemployed (though you need not be actually receiving benefit to qualify), because they are paid for by the DFEE. The budgets are limited and have been cut in recent years, which is one reason why you may find that you cannot get on a course which otherwise seems to fit you absolutely.

Courses at further education colleges

Courses at further education colleges are free to people on social security benefits or Housing Benefit, and there may be an alternative low income test. At Newcastle College, for example, you qualify under this if your income is below £14,000. Otherwise, you will have to pay course fees, which vary considerably between courses. Other colleges and providers may also offer their courses free to those on social security benefits, or charge a reduced rate; it is always worth enquiring.

Degree-level courses

If you haven't already had a local education authority grant at some time in your life for doing a degree-level course, you may still be able to get one. Some courses are 'mandatory', which means that grants have to be paid to students on that course who qualify on financial grounds. Others, such as some professional courses, are 'discretionary', which means that in many cases the local authority will no longer even consider them.

However, grants do not represent wealth these days (the basic 1995–96 levels are £2,340 in London and £1,885 elsewhere), and you will need extra help as well. The Student Loan Company gives interest-free loans, but it has recently been bedevilled by delays and maladministration. But loans are not provided to people over the age of 50, presumably because they consider that you may not have the time to pay them back. There are also some Access Funds for people in special hardship.

A free leaflet about student grants and loans is published by the DFEE. There is also a special guide for mature students, called Stepping Up, produced by UCAS, the universities admission service (see 'Useful publications').

Career Development Loans

An alternative method of financing yourself is a Career Development Loan (CDL). These started in 1988, with the objective of 'encouraging individuals to take greater responsibility for their vocational training'.

They are run by four of the clearing banks for the DFEE. You can apply for a loan of between £200 and £8,000 to pay 80 per cent of the course fees and associated expenses, including the cost of books and materials (and living expenses for full-time courses).

You normally still have to cover the remaining 20 per cent of the cost yourself. If you have been unemployed for more than three months, however, you can receive 100 per cent if the TEC/LEC approves the course. TECs and LECs also have the discretion to offer top-up grants to cover the remaining 20 per cent or to reduce the cost of borrowing.

There are various eligibility rules for CDLs, including the following:

▶ You must not be receiving other funding which covers the expenses applied for.

▶ You must be without access to funds to pay for the training course without a CDL.

▶ You must intend to use the training for work in the UK or elsewhere in the European Union.

Courses can be full-time, part-time or distance learning, but they must not last more than two years.

You do not have to start paying back the loan until a month after you have finished the training period, and the DFEE also pays the interest up to this point. If you are still unemployed after this, you can defer repayment for a further five months. Once you start paying it back, the terms and interest rates are much like any other unsecured loan.

Take-up of these loans is much lower than the Government had hoped, despite advertising campaigns. According to Margaret McPhail of Tyneside Careers, 'People see them as very much a last resort. If you are doing a lengthy course, you may need to borrow thousands of pounds, and people generally don't want to get into that sort of debt.' They are, nevertheless, worth considering for something that will definitely improve your career prospects.

If you have a lump-sum payment from leaving your previous job, you could also invest this in training or education.

If you are financing yourself, and can't afford a full-time course, doing it part-time or on a distance learning basis may be cheaper, and could allow you to earn some income at the same time.

Learning while unemployed

The position for those wanting to study part-time while signing on as unemployed is complicated. Essentially, it's heavily discouraged unless it's a course within the Training for Work system.

If you are sent on a Training for Work course, you receive a 'Participation Allowance' equal to your rate of social security benefits plus £10 per week (or only the £10 if you are not entitled to benefits). Otherwise you have to meet two different tests to decide whether you are still eligible for benefit. First, if you are claiming Unemployment Benefit/Jobseeker's Allowance or National Insurance contribution credits you have to show the Employment Service that you are still available for and actively seeking work. This will usually mean filling in a lengthy questionnaire and attending an interview. The Employment Service advisers' instructions are that claimants

▶ must show that they are available to start work immediately;

▶ must not place restrictions on the work they are available to do, which would leave them with no real prospect of finding a job;

▶ must take steps each week that give them the best prospect of finding a job.

Benefit will automatically be suspended until a ruling is given if you have paid a fee of more than £100 for the course, or if it leads to a qualification that you need for the job you are looking for. (This seems absurd; presumably the rationale is that you won't be serious about finding that job until you have finished the course.)

If your benefit is removed as a result of this test, you *may* be eligible for Income Support (if you meet all the other requirements). Here the rules are different. You can still receive benefit if you are doing a course for less than 21 hours 'guided learning hours' a week (16 hours from April 1996). The course must be run by a college, school or equivalent, and you must have been receiving benefit for at least three months immediately before it started. You must also be prepared to stop the course as soon as a suitable job becomes available.

Points to think about

Outside London, it may be difficult to find the course you want close enough to home to be practical. 'If people want to do art therapy, for instance,' says Margaret McPhail, 'the only two courses are in Sheffield and Edinburgh. That's going to be difficult for anyone who's got family commitments. Travelling, or living away from home for a period, is more likely to be a barrier for women than for men.'

Even if you can face the upheaval, the costs you will have to meet may be too high. So you may need to think again about what you want to do, and decide how determined you are. If you have set your heart on a particular career, and this is the only route to it, then you will need to grit your teeth and work out a way of doing it. If it is one of several things you are interested in, or a slightly different course will also help you achieve your aims, then think about doing that instead. Distance learning – where you are based at home and are in contact with your tutors through the post (or the computer), with perhaps a few residential sessions each year – may be the answer. The Open University, and many other universities and colleges, provide courses on this basis.

There is no need to struggle with these decisions on your own. Help from trained guidance workers is available, and you should take advantage of it.

CHAPTER NINE

Organising your time and other commitments

If you were employed for a long period before your current job finished, the idea of organising your own timetable from now on probably seems both attractive and daunting. Unless you step straight into another full-time job, you will have new spaces in your day and no fixed pattern for filling them; at the same time you will have new commitments to meet. What these are will depend on what your position is, and so they will change as your own pattern of activity changes. But you will also find that other people have new expectations of you – some that you appreciate and some that you do not.

The major issues – and the adjustment process that has to go on – will tend to differ between men and women. A woman with a family still at home, or with elderly relatives living close by, may find an expectation among her family that once she has left her job she will simply stay at home and 'housekeep'. The demands put on her time may build up quite rapidly, on the assumption that she has nothing better to do; she may then find it quite difficult to pursue her own projects.

If you are a man who has always been at work, on the other hand, the family perhaps won't make the same demands on you. Quite rightly, though, there is likely to be an expectation that you will do *something* in the home. You may find it difficult to cope with this. You may find yourself spending more time with your family than you have done for many years, except on holiday, and this too will take some getting used to.

One of the warnings often given to men is that they should not start trying to reorganise and manage the home. It has got on perfectly well without them so far, so why should it be changed? There can be irritations all round as different people within the family adapt. It would usually be better to fit in and take on a fair share of the routine tasks rather than create a major upheaval.

It will help you to work all these problems out if you make a sensible and constructive plan about how you will use your time and negotiate that with the rest of your family. This chapter looks at some of the points to think about:

▶ during the job search process;

▶ when starting a new job;

▶ when starting to work from home;

▶ when coping with caring responsibilities;

▶ when you have undertaken a 'portfolio' of activities.

Hunting for a job

A job search is a *serious* project, quite time-consuming and possibly stressful. You need to plan and allocate time accordingly. It is a project that you could need to undertake more than once, because the first job you get may be only temporary, it may not suit you, or it may not be what you want as time goes on and your financial position and other commitments change.

Whatever type of work you are looking for, the commitment is going to be much the same. It is a full-time job looking for work these days, whether full-time or part-time.

Chapter 5 looked at the practical steps to be taken. Just as important, though, is working out how to use your time and energy effectively on the project. To quote the authors of the BBC Handbook *Making Time:* 'Like every plan of campaign you must have objectives and targets to aim for. If you don't know where you are going it is highly unlikely you will get there – or know if you have arrived.'

If you are claiming the Jobseeker's Allowance (explained on pp 116–118), you will be required to sign a Jobseeker's Agreement committing you to a certain plan of action. Treat it as a framework in which to fit your job-hunting activities.

Problems with managing your time

Particular problems with managing your time that *Making Time* highlights are:

The lack of framework or structure to your day You have been used to getting up early and dashing off to catch a bus or train, and then getting back home again at the same time each evening with barely enough time to eat before dashing off to a leisure activity. Now – especially if you are feeling rather depressed about the whole experience – there may seem to be no good reason to get up at any particular hour, and too little to do to fill your time.

The lack of a support system In the past, you may have relied heavily on colleagues, especially if you were in a position where you had staff to whom you could delegate tasks. You may not even have known how to work the photocopier or the coffee machine, if someone else always did it for you. Now the only coffee machine is the one you switch on, and the photocopier is in the newsagents down the road, if you are lucky.

The impact on your family They won't be used to seeing you at home, and may feel that now you have all this free time, you could just carry out this or that chore without trouble. If your partner has unexpectedly become the sole breadwinner, you will both have problems adjusting.

A reversion to traditional patterns, with one partner in a couple 'housekeeping' while the other goes out to work, is a luxury many of us would like but few can afford these days. But if your partner is expecting this, there could be tensions.

So make it plain to yourself and others that you are going to devote your ordinary working hours to your job search, and avoid having them eaten into by other activities. But since you are no longer travelling to work, there will still be extra time available for doing housework or spending with the family as well.

Set yourself targets

Making Time suggests setting a target time, say three months, and then breaking that down into weeks during which you carry out specific tasks such as writing and revising your CV, drawing up a contacts list and following up a certain number each day, and visiting trade exhibitions to keep up to date with events. Draw up a daily 'Things to do' list, it suggests – and then actually do them!

A work discipline is especially important for the tasks you hate doing. No one really likes phoning up to pursue contacts or applications. Even the most extrovert person goes shy at the thought that their 'contact' may have forgotten altogether who she or he is. So, *Making Time* suggests, set aside, say, four 15-minute stints a day for the phone calls you don't want to make. (*Always* keep a note of who you have phoned, or who has phoned you, and what was said – it is extremely easy to confuse two conversations in your mind.)

Writing yourself a list of things you need to do means that you will go to the Jobclub or the reference library to deal with specific tasks, rather than just dropping in to while away time.

Review the situation

Once you are organised, don't just let your search drift on and become a routine in itself. One adviser has a client who has been coming in to the office regularly for two and a half years. Perhaps he was unlucky, but he could also have been looking for the wrong type of job or in the wrong place.

Review the way you are working, and your progress, regularly. If things don't seem to be working out, think about whether your original plans were realistic, and whether you are going about things in the right way. Talk it over with someone else such as the Careers Service if you can. If you are claiming Unemployment Benefit (Jobseeker's Allowance from October 1996), they will probably require reviews at intervals in any case, with the aim of persuading you to downgrade your expectations.

Starting a new job

When you start a new job – whether full-time or part-time – you may well find yourself in a very different environment from where you last worked. If you came out of a large organisation, you are now far more likely to be working in a small one, perhaps a small business or a partnership. If you have taken on a less taxing job, or one in a new field, you could also find that you are now a subordinate where before you were in charge (and you may not think much of the people to whom you are subordinated, either).

On top of that, there is the 'new child at school' syndrome: you don't know where everything is and what the office customs are. Even if people mean to be helpful, they may simply forget that you don't know what time the coffee break is, or the details of the National Lottery syndicate.

Starting in a new place is never easy, but you can help yourself by:

▶ thinking through some of the issues in advance, for instance how you will react if your boss is younger than you, and perhaps of the opposite sex when you were used to a single-sex environment;

▶ asking what you need to know (even if you are not given a proper induction course) and then writing down the details so you don't forget them;

▶ biting your tongue when it wants to start saying 'In my old job we did . . .' It is irritating for others and will make them feel that you are less flexible than you suggested in the interview.

If you think that the way they did something at your last workplace was better, why not suggest it as if it is your own idea and take the credit? You can always own up later if your conscience is troubling you!

Some workplaces appoint a 'mentor' for a new person, or people may informally take on the same role. If there is such a person, ask for a review meeting once you have been there a week, and then again a few weeks later, to establish how you are doing and what improvements (if any) you could make in your work.

You may also need to spend a little time working out the best route to work. Give yourself the space to prepare properly; try your route by public transport the week before you start work, for instance.

Check on the dress conventions if you can, or otherwise arrive looking as smart as you think can possibly be required on the first day, and dress down on future days if it turns out not to be necessary.

If you are being paid at the end of the month, and this will leave a gap in your finances, then ask the employer for a 'sub' to tide you over, or get a short-term overdraft from the bank. Check if you can get a loan for a season ticket, for instance.

Starting to work from home

Organising your time when working from home, whether as a self-employed person or in some form of telework, is one of the most difficult things to get right. It is not easy to control the flow of work, and this can result in periods when you hardly have time to turn around, and feel that you cannot possibly chase another order. But the result of that, a few months later, is a work famine, when you have to spend a lot of time chasing work and so cannot earn what you need.

Again the answer is to organise your time properly, and make the space for the necessary but tedious chores. There may also be some office skills that, if you have them, will cut down immensely on the time that things will take – such as typing/word processing and using computer spreadsheets and databases. Your local TEC/LEC or a college of further education may be able to offer relevant training (see pp 96–98).

Set yourself targets

The authors of *Making Time* suggest that the first step is to set yourself some objectives, in fairly concrete terms. In Chapter 3 it was suggested that you should work out your income requirements on a monthly or weekly basis, so that gives you a clear target to aim for. You can then assess how many products/contracts/assignments that means.

Next, they suggest, make yourself a chart of monthly, weekly and daily targets and keep them under your nose at all times. Keep referring to your plan: tick off what you achieve, and change the targets if they are too hard or too easy. 'Make sure you include all the activities you need to do in order to achieve your goals; remember the things you don't like doing but know you must.'

Include in this the time you will need to get your contacts and support system set up, which can be surprisingly lengthy. You may need to allow time for any or all of the following:

▶ sorting out a bank or building society account;

▶ VAT registration;

▶ getting planning permission;

▶ notifying the tax office;

▶ arranging to pay Class 2 (self-employed) National Insurance contributions;

▶ seeing Business Link counsellors and attending training courses (see p 74);

▶ getting hold of the right equipment;

▶ taking out subscriptions to magazines, or finding where you can get access to them;

▶ buying office equipment and stationery.

It is necessary to invest in the proper equipment to do the job – though not to spend extravagantly on it. Second-hand office equipment is perfectly adequate, but you will need filing cabinets and shelving if your work is likely to generate paper.

Find space and time away from your family

You also need to create office or workshop space. If you take over the sitting room there will be friction with your family but, equally, you won't do yourself justice if you perch on a corner of the kitchen table with other activities going on around you. You need some exclusive space for your work, even if it is the boxroom or part of your bedroom, but you also need to leave your family their own space.

Finding time in your own home may also mean some thought and negotiation. Teenagers who are never off the phone, or who wander into the sitting room looking dishevelled when you have a client there, don't help with the starting up of any business. You can to some extent adjust your working times to fit in with the realities of home life, but you will also need to work out some rules together and then stick to them.

If you live on your own

If you live on your own, rather than in a family, you may find the opposite problem: that you never stop working. When your office or workspace is in your own home, it is too easy to carry on tinkering away all the time and never take a real break. The quality of your work will suffer, though, if you let yourself do this.

Set yourself definite working times, with gaps between them when you go for a walk, make coffee, eat a genuine sit-down meal and so on. Build in time when you see friends and indulge in leisure activities. Occasionally you will have to break this pattern, when you are asked to do something in a rush and it can't be completed in any other way but by working all hours, but that should be the exception rather than the rule.

Allow time for marketing, invoicing and preparing your work

Initially, much of your time will be spent marketing yourself and your services. As your business develops, you will need to spend rather less time on this, but the requirement will never go away. Even when you are at your busiest, you have to keep on thinking about where the next chunk of work will come from, and go out and find it if it does not arrive on your doorstep.

Set yourself a definite number of tasks to do each day – 'two phone calls and two follow-up letters to prospective customers' – or make yourself some rules, however arbitrary, about when and how to do marketing.

You will probably have to spend quite a lot of (unpaid) time discussing possibilities, making presentations and drawing up estimates. Though it will vary between different types of work, a good rule of thumb is that no more than half the people who say they are interested in you will actually follow it up, and no more than half of them will turn into serious customers. So the more regular customers you can build up, for whom there is no need to spend time introducing yourself and explaining what you can do, the better from this point of view.

After the work is done, you again need to set aside time to send in invoices, and then chase up anyone who does not pay. Another good rule of thumb is that the larger the organisation, the slower it will be at paying its bills!

Finally, when allocating time for the work you have taken on, don't forget about preparation time. It is easy to skimp on this now and then, but disastrous in the long run. If you are teaching a course, for instance, you can expect to spend as long writing the material, or doing major revisions, as running the course itself. The standard of presentation is becoming steadily more important (sometimes, one feels, at the expense of the content). So give yourself time to do things properly. Reflect it in the amount you charge.

Coping with caring responsibilities

This section is only a very brief look at a very big subject. There are about 6 million people who provide some care for someone who is disabled or elderly, whether in their own home or elsewhere. Many of them are in paid employment at the same time, including 750,000 people who provide care for more than 20 hours a week while holding down a paid job. (See the ACE Books publication *Caring in a Crisis: Choices for the carer of an elderly relative* or contact the Carers National Association (see 'Useful addresses') for much more information on this.)

You may find that when your work situation changes, you are asked, or expected, to take on the care of a relative or partner. Or you may already have been spending a substantial amount of time caring when you were in your previous employment. Either way, caring can be strenuous and stressful, especially if you are combining it with paid work.

Don't feel you have to manage on your own; there *is* help and support available, though it is not always easy to find out what there is. As Marina Lewycka says in *Choices for the carer of an elderly relative*:

'One of the things many carers find most difficult is getting the information they need. Whether you want to know more about what benefits you are entitled to or what care services are available, or whether you want to find out more about your relative's medical condition, it's important not to let yourself be fobbed off. . . . Be persistent. If you receive no satisfactory answer, ask again.'

Your GP and the social services department are the places to start looking for help. You may also find that there are local specialist services run by voluntary organisations (for instance 'sitters' provided by the Alzheimer's Disease Society). There are also many carers' support groups (some with paid staff) around the country. It can help ease the strain considerably just to sit down and talk to people with the same sort of problems as yourself. Contact the Carers National Association or the National Self-Help Support Centre for details of groups in your area (see the 'Useful addresses' section).

Aids and adaptations in the home and training – for instance in the best way to lift a bed-bound person – can also make life easier. Ask the GP or social services.

If you are going to cope, you will need time for yourself, however little, to go out and pursue your own interests. You may need to be quite assertive to ensure that your needs, as well as those of the person you are caring for, are taken into account.

It may be that you will come under pressure to do more than you want, or feel capable of doing, to save money on the social services budget. You are perfectly entitled to resist this: you have a life to lead as well. It will be easier to do this if you have planned out your own time already, and know what you can reasonably offer.

Some employers may offer family leave, paid or unpaid, to help with caring responsibilities. But there is no legal right to this in the UK. In the USA some employers are offering workplace day centres for their employees' elderly or disabled relatives, and a few employers in the UK are experimenting with a similar system. Keep your eyes out for any such arrangements in your area.

Benefits for carers

You may qualify for **Invalid Care Allowance (ICA)** if you spend a substantial amount of your time caring for a person with a disability (£36.60 per week in 1996–97). The first condition is that the person being cared for is receiving the care component of Disability Living Allowance at the middle or highest rate, or Attendance Allowance if they are over pension age. (Details of these are not covered here; see DSS leaflets DS 704 and

HB 6, or DS 702, or ACE Books annual publication *Your Rights: A guide to money benefits for older people.*

If this condition is satisfied, then the carer will be entitled to ICA if he or she is:

▶ not gainfully employed or in full-time education (this means that they earn less than £50 after deduction of reasonable expenses, or are on a course that involves fewer than 21 hours of supervised study – 16 hours from April 1996);

▶ 'regularly and substantially' caring – this means caring for 35 hours a week or more;

▶ aged between 16 and 65.

ICA is taxable (except for any child addition). You also receive Class 1 National Insurance credits towards your pension.

Doing a mixture of activities

You may have found yourself taking on a 'portfolio' of activities including part-time employment, self-employment, perhaps a college course, perhaps caring and family commitments. Women who have brought up families in the past will probably find it easier to juggle the time spent on these various elements than men. But for everyone, it is important to organise your life well and exercise great self-discipline so that you don't run yourself into the ground and become unreliable.

As with looking for a job or working from home, the essential is to set up the space and time *at home* to enable you to do the things you are committed to. Plan out what you are doing and when. Draw up a weekly timetable of when you are supposed to be where, taking account of travelling time, preparation (especially important for learning and teaching activities) and administration. Get a wall calendar with space to write on, and fill it in each weekend for the following week. Get your spouse/partner and the rest of your family to do the same, so you each know where the others are.

Press the rest of the family to take on a fair share of household responsibilities, if they haven't done so in the past. But there is anyway no need to feel that you have to be Superwoman (or man): a bit of dust on the skirting board never hurt anyone.

If one element seems to be squeezing out the others, think about the reasons for it and what can be adjusted. You may need to renegotiate some of the arrangements. This may be particularly necessary with family commitments, which can be very demanding.

CHAPTER TEN

Financial issues

Once you have finished your job and started another pattern of life, your financial arrangements will clearly change. The resources available to you may be less than they were before – or they could be more – but they will come from different places. This chapter looks at the various State benefits you may qualify for while you are unemployed, if you are sick, or if your income is below a certain level.

It also looks at replacing the non-wage benefits you would have had from your employer and at what to do if money problems arise.

Claiming State benefits when unemployed

You may find that you are out of a job only for a short time, while you sort out your other arrangements. Or it may be rather longer, if things don't work out quite as you had planned and the opportunities don't seem to turn up. In this case you may well have to sign on as unemployed, and this means fitting in with the Government's rules.

Unemployment Benefit

Up until October 1996, the National Insurance benefit for unemployed people is Unemployment Benefit (£48.25 per week in 1996–97). As long as you have paid enough National Insurance contributions, it is paid for up to a year and can include an addition for a non-working spouse.

To qualify, you need to show that you are available for work and that you are actively seeking work. You claim Unemployment Benefit from an Unemployment Benefit Office – not always the same place as the Jobcentre. You need to sign on, usually once a fortnight, and you will be called in for interviews at the beginning of your period of unemployment and at different points after that. You can claim for yourself even if your spouse is working. If you have an occupational or personal pension of more than £35, and you are over 55 years of age, your Unemployment Benefit will be restricted by £1 for each £1 above that figure (if your occupational pension is £45, for instance, you lose £10 of your benefit). There is also a rule that if you left your job 'voluntarily and without just cause' or because of 'misconduct' you can be disqualified from benefit for up to six months.

If you have lost your job because of a compulsory redundancy, or the closure of the workplace or the firm, this should not apply to you. If you took *voluntary* redundancy, the Employment Service may try to apply the rule, but they should not. Essentially, if the employer was looking for volunteers to make up a certain number of redundancies, and would have made it compulsory if enough volunteers did not come forward, you are not voluntarily unemployed (see *Unemployment and Training Rights Handbook*, in 'Useful publications', for more information).

On the other hand, if you chose to take early retirement and were not put under pressure to do so, you would normally be assumed to be voluntarily unemployed. But if the employer had made things intolerable for you, or if there were urgent family reasons, these could count as 'just cause'. If you feel the rule is being unfairly applied to you, exercise your right of appeal to a Social Security Appeal Tribunal.

Jobseeker's Allowance

From October 1996, Jobseeker's Allowance (JSA) replaces Unemployment Benefit. For the first six months, JSA will be paid on the basis of the National Insurance contributions you have made, and then on a means-tested basis (that is, taking both your capital and your income into account). The non-means-tested element will cover only the individual claimant, however, and not his or her family, so many people will need to start claiming means-tested JSA immediately.

If you have capital of more than £8,000, you will not be entitled to claim means-tested JSA (even if your weekly income is low), so then you will receive JSA for six months only and no State benefits thereafter.

If you have a pension (whether from an employer or a personal pension) of more than £50 a week, JSA will be deducted pound for pound over that figure. The rules on voluntary unemployment and misconduct, explained above, will stay the same as for Unemployment Benefit.

If your spouse or partner works 24 hours a week or more, there will be no entitlement to means-tested JSA (though you might be eligible for Family Credit).

Anyone wanting to claim JSA will be required to be available for any work which they can reasonably be expected to do. You will be expected to be available for a minimum of 40 hours a week, but if you are offered suitable work for fewer hours you will be expected to accept it. You will be able to refuse a job, or restrict the hours of availability, only

▶ on grounds of health;

▶ for religious and conscientious reasons;

▶ to meet caring responsibilities.

You must be available to start work immediately, unless you are doing voluntary work without payment or are a carer, when 48 hours' notice is allowed. For a 'permitted period' of up to 13 weeks, you will be able to restrict your job search to self-employment. You will also be able to refuse jobs which are vacant because of trade disputes (strikes or lock-outs).

You will also have to show that you are 'actively seeking work', and all claimants will have to sign a Jobseeker's Agreement, committing them to a certain plan of action. This, the Government says, 'will involve activities at various stages, probably becoming more intensive as the period of unemployment goes on'.

A typical example could involve someone attending a Jobclub, then going on a training course; if still unemployed, they might then be referred to Community Action. (This is a temporary employment scheme introduced in 1993, which offers long-term unemployed people part-time work 'of value to the community', linked with support with job-seeking.) If anyone disputes the relevance of the options, they can be given a Jobseeker's Direction making it compulsory as a condition of receiving benefit.

If your health is not good

There are people who are not well – perhaps have not been for a long time – but who have found it possible to manage their job in an environment which they know and where people are sympathetic. There are people who have struggled through their work each day but have been completely exhausted by the time they get home and collapse into bed at six o'clock. A person with back problems, for example, might have had their work rearranged by management or sympathetic colleagues to ensure that they did not have to do heavy lifting. Once you are on the wider labour market, this may not be possible and you could find that the will to carry on has gone.

Incapacity Benefit

Talk to your GP about whether you would qualify for the new Incapacity Benefit, and get a copy of the form and the 'scoresheet' (explained below) to see how far you would meet the new tests. It is also worth checking to see whether you could qualify for an ill-health pension under your own pension scheme's rules, rather than an ordinary early retirement pension.

If you are receiving Statutory Sick Pay (SSP) at the time when your job ends, or if you become sick when you are unemployed, you will need to claim Incapacity Benefit, on the lowest rate to start with (see p 120 for information on the different rates). The fact that you are already claiming Unemployment Benefit (Jobseeker's Allowance from October 1996) does *not* stop you claiming Incapacity Benefit if you fall ill or if a condition you already had worsens.

However, if you claim Incapacity Benefit when you are unemployed you immediately become subject to the 'all-work' test. The aim of this is to decide whether, on a supposedly objective test of the extent to which your illness or disability impairs your performance of certain physical and mental functions, you are capable of work. There is no reference to your last job, and no account is taken of education or training, or of any language or literacy problems.

Some people are exempt from this test. The main groups are:

▶ those who are terminally ill;

▶ those who are registered as blind;

▶ those whom the DSS doctors agree are suffering from one of a list of illnesses, including the effects of a stroke, AIDS, dementia, the advanced stages of multiple sclerosis or Parkinson's disease (but there could still be disputes about whether or not the diagnosis is correct);

▶ those who are getting the highest rate of the care component of Disability Living Allowance.

(This is a summary; for the full list see DSS leaflet IB 202.)

The 'all-work' test is a test of the ability to perform the activities set out in the regulations. There are two lists, one of physical disabilities and one of mental disabilities. Each contains categories of activity. The physical disabilities list includes such activities as 'walking up and down stairs', 'bending and kneeling', 'reaching' and 'continence'. The mental disabilities list includes activities such as 'daily living' and 'coping with pressure'.

For each activity there is then a further list of 'descriptors'. These describe possible levels of disability within the area of the activity, each of which carries points. For the ability to walk up and down stairs, for example, the descriptors are:

Cannot walk up and down one stair	15 points
Cannot walk up and down a flight of 12 stairs	15 points
Cannot walk up and down a flight of 12 stairs without holding on and taking a rest	7 points
Can walk up and down a flight of 12 stairs only if going sideways or one step at a time	3 points
No problem in walking up and down stairs	0 points

To be treated as incapable of work, you have to score a total of *either* 15 points from the physical disabilities list *or* 10 points from the mental disabilities list. There is a complicated arrangement for translating mental disabilities points into physical disabilities points for those with problems in both areas.

If you score too few points on this test, you can still be treated as incapable of work if a doctor working for the Benefits Agency Medical Service (BAMS) accepts that:

▶ You are suffering from a previously undiagnosed, potentially life-threatening condition (such as heart disease).

▶ You have a disease or disablement which means that there would be a substantial risk to the health of any person (including yourself) if you were found capable of work.

▶ You suffer from a severe uncontrolled or uncontrollable disease.

▶ You are to undergo a major operation or other major therapeutic procedure within the next three months.

To apply, you fill in a lengthy questionnaire (form IB 50). If there is any doubt about your condition, you are called up for an examination by the DSS's own medical advisers (the BAMS). Your own GP will be asked to give information and to release your medical records (with your permission), but does not have any other role.

Anyone who disputes the DSS decision can appeal to a Social Security Appeal Tribunal. In practice, it is difficult to win here unless you turn up in person and can supply additional written evidence from your GP or consultant. While you are waiting for an appeal to be heard, you will not be paid Incapacity Benefit and may need to claim Income Support.

There are three basic rates of Incapacity Benefit:

▶ First 28 weeks of sickness (if not getting SSP): short-term lower rate (no increases for children).

▶ From 29 to 52 weeks: short-term higher rate.

▶ After one year: long-term rate.

Very disabled people, or those with a terminal illness, receive the long-term rate from week 29.

There is also an age-related allowance, paid with the long-term rate, where the person was under 45 on the first day of their present illness and a larger allowance for those under 35 at the start. Adult dependency increases will be paid only where the spouse is aged 60 or over, or caring for a child for whom you are getting a child increase (so not with the short-term lower rate). There is also an earnings rule for adult dependants which means that if they earn more than a certain amount no increase will be paid.

The short-term higher rate of benefit and the long-term rate are both taxable. This means that for people with enough other income to make them liable to pay tax, the short-term higher rate is actually worth less than the lower rate.

Industrial injuries benefits

If you feel that your ill-health has been caused by an accident at work, or is the result of a disease that you picked up at work, it will be worth checking whether you are entitled to industrial injuries benefits.

These can be paid where an employee has had an accident 'arising out of and in the course of employment' or where he or she is suffering from a 'prescribed disease'. That means an illness which is on a DSS list in relation to the particular occupation in which you worked. It covers, for instance, a number of cancers and skin diseases, occupational deafness (but only for a certain number of occupations), some chest diseases, and some types of work-related limb disorders.

The main form of industrial injuries benefit is **Disablement Benefit**, paid either for a limited period or for life, if your industrial disease or injury is serious enough. The payments can be made *on top* of wages or other benefits. There are also some additional benefits for very badly disabled people.

There is also a **Reduced Earnings Allowance** (REA), though this is now limited to cases where the accident happened, or the disease arose, before October 1990. If you are already claiming REA, or are changing or leaving your job because you are now permanently incapable of employment of the same standard as before, it will be worth checking whether there is anything extra to come from this source.

All industrial injuries benefits are non-contributory, so they cover all 'employed earners', including married women paying reduced-rate National Insurance contributions. They can act as a passport to other benefits. They are quite separate from the right to sue the employer in the courts for negligence (but if you win a damages award, the DSS will reclaim the benefit it has paid out).

If you think that you might be able to claim an industrial injuries benefit, talk to your union or staff association if you have one, or the Citizens Advice Bureau if not.

Married women and National Insurance benefits

If you are a married woman or widow, you may have been paying the reduced-rate National Insurance contribution (still described as the 'small stamp' by many people) of 3.85 per cent of your earnings. The only thing that this qualifies you for, in your own right, is industrial injuries benefits, as explained above. For everything else, you are treated simply as your husband's dependant, so you can't claim Unemployment Benefit (Jobseeker's Allowance from October 1996) or Incapacity Benefit for yourself, even if you would otherwise qualify.

If you have a break in employment of two complete consecutive tax years, you will need to pay full-rate NI contributions when you go back to work. But if the gap is shorter than that, you can still retain your 'election' to pay at the reduced rate.

Means-tested benefits

If you find that you do not have enough money to live on, there are means-tested benefits for which you may be eligible, though not while you have capital over a certain limit. These include:

Income Support, if neither you nor your spouse/partner works for less than 16 hours a week.

Family Credit or **Disability Working Allowance (DLA)** if either you or your spouse/partner works more than 16 hours a week.

Housing Benefit and **Council Tax Benefit**.

In order to claim Income Support, Family Credit or DWA, an individual or couple must have no more than £8,000 capital; for Housing Benefit and Council Tax Benefit the limit is £16,000. So if your income is low and you have less capital than the limit (or if you are spending a redundancy or severance payment in order to live, and your capital has come down to that level), it is worth checking if you are eligible. Any occupational pension is taken into account, and a 'tariff' income of £1 per week for every £250 of savings that you have over £3,000. Ask the Citizens Advice Bureau, or the local council's welfare rights officer if there is one. For more information see ACE Books annual publication *Your Rights* or the Child Poverty Action Group's *National Welfare Benefits Handbook*, also published annually.

Your mortgage

Mortgage insurance

If you have redundancy insurance on your mortgage, check out what you have to do about it before you leave work, if possible, and make sure that you get the right documents. You may need a letter or statement from your employer making it clear that it is their choice rather than yours that you are leaving.

Mortgage insurance is notorious for the small print in the policies which reduces the chance of payouts. The Director-General of the Council of Mortgage Lenders himself said not long ago that it was 'not really worth a great deal'. So you may have some trouble extracting payments from your insurance company, and need to fight. Again, the Citizens Advice Bureau, or a money advice agency if there is one locally, should be able to help.

Income Support

Since October 1995, there have been new rules on the payment of Income Support to help with mortgage interest. Assuming that you already had a mortgage before the rules changed, you will get no help with the payments for the first two months, and only 50 per cent for the next four months. (If you first took out the mortgage after 1 October

1995, the delay will be nine months, though there are exceptions for some groups.)

There is also a top limit on the size of mortgage that can be covered, again with some exceptions. The limit has been gradually reduced, and now stands at £100,000. If you have a redundancy or severance payment, you may need to use it to pay your mortgage – perhaps repaying some of the capital as well. Talk to your building society or other lender about this. If there is a danger of your falling into arrears, explain the situation as early as possible, and ask for help in rescheduling the payments if possible.

Getting into debt

Sadly, this can happen even when you have had a substantial pay-off from your employer. It could be the largest lump sum you have ever seen, and you may feel it is inexhaustible; some people do feel the urge to 'spend, spend, spend'. Mortgage or credit card arrears are perhaps the most common problem that arises; mortgage arrears can be particularly serious because people can lose their homes as a result.

Many people who are getting into debt are paralysed by it, and stop opening letters for fear that they will be bills or summonses. This is actually the worst thing you can do; the best thing is to talk to an informed adviser (try the Citizens Advice Bureau or a money advice centre), and get their help with writing to all your creditors explaining the situation and sorting out an organised way in which you can pay off the arrears. See *Rights Guide for Home Owners* and the *Debt Advice Handbook* (see 'Useful publications') for suggestions about what to do. If you can't find a local agency that can help, the National Debtline (see 'Useful addresses') will be able to give you some assistance.

Replacing non-wage benefits from your old employer

This section looks briefly at some of the benefits you may have had from your old employer, which you may not have in your new pattern of activity. Small employers tend to provide a much less generous package of benefits than large ones, and part-time and casual workers have often been excluded from benefits (though this has had to change to some extent, because of European law). And of course if you are self-employed, studying or doing unpaid voluntary work you will not have an employer to provide benefits anyway.

A car

If you have lost the use of a company car, it may be vital (or simply necessary for your current lifestyle) to replace it. This would be one use of any redundancy or severance payment; but think when you are buying about maintenance costs and insurance. People with company cars are sheltered from the impact of these, and they may come as a nasty shock.

If you have a good driving record, and few or no claims on the company's car insurance, you will want to ensure that this is carried over into your own policy. Find out from the company who the insurers or brokers are, and talk to them about doing this. Although in the past it would have been quite a rare request, it is now much more common and they should be able to deal with it. Otherwise, if you have a trade union or professional body, it is worth checking out if they offer any special deals.

Look around for insurers who give better rates to older motorists. Several companies offer such policies, including Age Concern Insurance Services (see 'Useful addresses').

Pension and death benefits

If a new employer provides these, it will almost always be worth joining the scheme (though not necessarily transferring your money from any previous scheme; that will depend on what is on offer from each). You may have to undergo a medical examination, and if your health is not good you could be refused entry, though that would be rare.

If you are working part-time for a new employer, the amount you and they are contributing, and the earnings on which the pension or death benefit will be based, could be low. You might want to start paying Additional Voluntary Contributions, up to the limit that you are allowed by the Inland Revenue, in order to build up a larger amount of pension.

For most people, the pension they have earned in one job need have no bearing on the amount of pension they can build up in the next job. But there are some exceptions for the higher paid, and those in very good pension schemes. Check with the new employer's Pensions Department if you fall into one of these categories; they will be able to tell you whether, as a result, you will have special limits applied to the maximum pension you can get in the new job.

The alternative, if there is no pension scheme available via your employer, is to take out a personal pension and your own life assurance. This will be expensive, because costs rise sharply as you get older, so work out what you can afford to spend without overcommitting yourself.

If you are self-employed, you will need to set up your own personal pension, as discussed on page 81. (See *The Pensions Handbook*, published annually by ACE Books, for more information on pensions.)

Unfortunately, if you are not employed – perhaps because you are studying or doing voluntary work – you will not be able to pay into a pension scheme as you have no earnings. But you could pay into a PEP or a TESSA, or simply set money aside in some form of savings, so that you can make the maximum contribution in years when you do have earnings.

Permanent health insurance

You may find that a new employer provides a decent sick pay scheme, or it may be Statutory Sick Pay only. There could also be a qualifying period before you are entitled to full benefits.

If a reasonable scheme is not available to you, then you may need to take out permanent health insurance (PHI) on your own account – though again, it is sadly expensive for older people, and especially for women. Self-employed people may also need to do this.

PHI pays up to three-quarters of your earnings, less any State and company benefits, if you are prevented from working through disability or long-term illness. Benefits are tax-free if you are paying the premiums yourself, and are paid as long as you qualify on health grounds, or until retirement age if that is earlier.

However, the policies tend to be full of small print conditions, so specialist independent advice is essential. Check out particularly whether the premium rate is 'reviewable' (which means that it can be increased without warning), what the definition of disability is, and what exclusions there are.

Useful publications

Age and Employment: Policies, attitudes and practices (1993) Institute of Personnel and Development. £35.

Career Development Loans, information pack and application form (CDL 1), free from DFEE Publications Centre, PO Box 2193, London E15 2EU.

Caring for Someone? (1995) Benefits Agency leaflet FB 31; free from local Benefits Agency offices.

Change at the Top: Working flexibly at senior and managerial levels in organisations (1993) New Ways to Work. £12.50.

Changing Your Job after 35 (1993) Godfrey Golzen and Philip Plumbley, Kogan Page. £8.99.

Debt Advice Handbook (1995) Child Poverty Action Group. £9.95.

Directory of Volunteering and Employment Opportunities (1995) Jan Brownfoot and Frances Wilks, Directory of Social Change. £9.95.

Disability Rights Handbook (published annually) Disability Alliance ERA. £8.95 (£5 for individuals receiving any State benefits).

Employment Handbook, ACAS; available from ACAS Reader Ltd, PO Box 16, Earl Shilton, Leicester LE9 8ZZ. £1.50 plus £1 postage.

European Directory of Career Management and Outplacement Consultants, Executive Grapevine, London. £28 + £2.50 postage.

Finding the Right Job (1994) Ann Segal with William Grierson, BBC Books. £4.99

The Good Retirement Guide (published annually) Kogan Page. £14.99.

Help at Hand: The home carers' survival guide (1990) Jane Brotchie, Bedford Square Press. £6.95.

Hired, Fired, or Sick and Tired (1995) Lynda Macdonald, Nicholas Brealey Publications. £9.99.

How to Set Up and Run Your Own Business, Daily Telegraph Business Enterprise Book (1995) Kogan Page. £9.99.

How to Work for a Charity (1994) Jan Brownfoot and Frances Wilks, Directory of Social Change. £7.95.

How We Can Help, Employment Service; free leaflet about claiming redundancy payments.

Job Hunter's Handbook (1994) David Greenwood, Kogan Page. £7.99.

Job Sharing: A practical guide (1990) Pam Walton, Kogan Page. £7.99.

Making Time (1993) Gerard Hargreaves, Dorothy Morfett and Geraldine Bown, BBC Books. £5.99.

National Welfare Benefits Handbook (published annually) Child Poverty Action Group. £7.95.

The New Guide to Working from Home (1995) Sue Read, Headline. £7.99.

Part-Time Work, Judith Humphries, Kogan Page (out of print).

Pay and Benefits Pocket Book (published annually) NTC Publications in association with Bacon and Woodrow. £19.95 + £1.50 postage.

Pay Your Way as a Student, Hobsons Publishing; available from Biblios PDS Ltd, Star Road, Partridge Green, West Sussex RH13 8LD. £7.99.

The Perfect CV (1991) Tom Jackson, Judy Piatkus (Publishers) Ltd. £9.95.

Postgraduate Awards, DFEE leaflet; free from DFEE Publications Centre, PO Box 2193, London E15 2EU.

Public Bodies (1994) Cabinet Office, HMSO. £13.

Redundancy Payments: A guide for employers, employees and others (PL 808), DTI; available from Jobcentres, CABs and libraries.

Rights Guide for Home Owners (1994) Paul Moorhouse and David Thomas, Child Poverty Action Group/SHAC. £7.95

Rights Guide to Non-Means Tested Benefits (published annually) Richard Poynter and Clive Martin, Child Poverty Action Group. £7.95.

Start a Successful Business (1994) Rosemary Phipps, BBC Books. £6.99.

Statement on Age and Employment (1993) Institute of Personnel and Development; free booklet.

Stepping Up: A mature student's guide to higher education, free from UCAS, Fulton House, Cheltenham, Glos GL50 3SH.

Student Grants and Loans: A brief guide for higher education students, DFEE booklet, free from DFEE Publications Centre, PO Box 2193, London E15 2EU.

Third Age Careers: Meeting the corporate challenge (1994) Barry Curnow and John McLean Fox, Gower. £28.50

Unemployment and Training Rights Handbook (1995) Dan Finn and Iain Murray, Unemployment Unit, London. £11.

Working for Charities, Charity Appointments, London; free booklet (Tel: 0171-247 4502).

Useful addresses

Advisory Conciliation and Arbitration Service (ACAS)
Public enquiry points in 11 cities in the UK (not Northern Ireland); numbers listed in every phone directory. Can help with advice and conciliation concerning your employment rights.

27 Wilton Street
London SW1X 7AZ
Tel: 0171-210 3000

Age Concern
For addresses of national organisations see page 135.

Age Concern Insurance Services
Acts as specialist brokers for insurance services for older people.

Garrod House
Chaldon Road
Caterham
Surrey CR3 5YZ
Tel: 01883 346964

Age Resource
The 'younger arm' of Age Concern, promoting the idea that active older people are an essential yet undervalued resource.

Astral House
1268 London Road
London SW16 4ER
Tel: 0181-679 8000
Direct line 0181-679 2201

British Association for Counselling
Can put you in touch with members who can offer counselling help.

1 Regent Place
Rugby
Warwickshire CV21 3BX
Tel: 01788 78328

British Association of Psychotherapists
Can put you in touch with members who can offer psychotherapy help.

121 Hendon Lane
London N3 3PR
Tel: 0181-347 1747

British Franchise Association
Provides help and advice on franchising opportunities.

Franchise Chambers
Thames View
Newtown Road
Henley on Thames
Oxon RG9 1HG
Tel: 01491 578049

Carers National Association
Gives information and support to people who are caring at home and produces a wide range of information leaflets.

20–25 Glasshouse Yard
London EC1A 4JS
Tel: 0171-490 8818
Helpline 0171-490 8898
(Monday–Friday 1–4.30 pm)

Contact a Family
Network of support groups for parents of children with special needs and disabilities. It has information and specialist groups for rare syndromes and genetic conditions.

16 Strutton Ground
London SW1P 2HP
Tel: 0171-222 2695

Department of Trade and Industry
Deals with queries about redundancy pay and how to make a claim.

Customer Service Unit
7th Floor
Hagley House
83–85 Hagley Road
Birmingham B16 8QG
Helpline 0800 84 84 89
Monday–Friday 9 am–5pm

Industrial Common Ownership Movement (ICOM)
Can offer advice and training to those wanting to set up a workers' co-op, or put you in touch with local sources of help.

Vassalli House
20 Central Road
Leeds LS1 6DE
Tel: 0113 249600

Institute of Personnel and Development (formerly Institute of Personnel Management)
The professional body for personnel and human resources managers; has produced a strong policy statement on age discrimination in employment.

IPD House
Camp Road
Wimbledon
London SW19 4UX
Tel: 0181-946 9100

National Association of Citizens Advice Bureaux
Information about your local Citizens Advice Bureau.

114–123 Pentonville Road
London N1 9LZ
Tel: 0171-833 2181

National Association of Councils for Voluntary Service (NACVS)
Can tell you about local Councils for Voluntary Service.

3rd Floor
Arundel Court
177 Arundel Street
Sheffield S1 2NU
Tel: 0114 2786636

National Association of Volunteer Bureaux
Can tell you if there is a Volunteer Bureau in your area.

St Peter's College
College Road
Saltley
Birmingham B8 3TE
Tel: 0121-327 0265

National Debtline
Can help with sorting out your financial affairs if you get badly into debt.

Birmingham Settlement
318 Summer Lane
Birmingham B19 8501
Tel: 0121-359 3562

National Self-Help Support Centre
Has a database of local and national groups for specified illnesses and disabilities.

26 Bedford Square
London WC1B 3HU
Tel: 0171-636 4066

National Volunteering Helpline
Can tell you what opportunities are available for volunteering in your area.

Tel: 0345 22 11 33
(calls charged at local rate)

New Ways to Work
Gives advice and assistance on job-sharing.

309 Upper Street
London N1 2TY
Tel: 0171-226 4026

Occupational Pensions Advisory Service (OPAS)

A voluntary organisation which gives advice and information on occupational and personal pensions and helps sort out problems.

11 Belgrave Road
London SW1V 1RB
Tel: 0171-233 8080

Pensions Ombudsman

Deals with complaints or disputes about occupational and personal pension schemes. The Ombudsman is appointed by the Government and is independent of the pension providers.

11 Belgrave Road
London SW1V 1RB
Tel: 0171-834 9144

Public Appointments Unit

Can put you on a panel of names to be considered for future public appointments.

(Cabinet Office)
Horseguards Road
London SW1T 3AL
Tel: 0171-270 6224

REACH

Places older people in voluntary work with charities.

Bear Wharf
27 Bankside
London SE1 9DP
Tel: 0171-928 0452

Working for a Charity

Runs courses on the ins and outs of working for a charity. Send an sae for details.

44–46 Caversham Road
London NW5 2DS
Tel: 0171-911 0353/
241 2091

About Age Concern

Changing Direction: Employment options in mid-life is one of a wide range of publications produced by Age Concern England, the National Council on Ageing. Age Concern England is actively engaged in training, information provision, fundraising and campaigning for older people and those who work with them, and also in the provision of products and services such as insurance for them.

A network of over 1,400 local Age Concern groups, with the support of around 250,000 volunteers, aims to improve the quality of life for older people and develop services appropriate to local needs and resources. These include advice and information, day care, visiting services, transport schemes, clubs, and specialist facilities for older people who are physically and mentally frail.

Age Concern England is a registered charity dependent on public support for the continuation and development of its work.

Age Concern England
1268 London Road
London SW16 4ER
Tel: 0181-679 8000

Age Concern Scotland
113 Rose Street
Edinburgh EH2 3DT
Tel: 0131-220 3345

Age Concern Cymru
4th Floor
1 Cathedral Road
Cardiff CF1 9SD
Tel: 01222 371566

Age Concern Northern Ireland
3 Lower Crescent
Belfast BT7 1NR
Tel: 01232 245729

Publications from ◆◉◆ Books

A wide range of titles is published by Age Concern England under the ACE Books imprint.

Employment

Earning Money in Retirement
Kenneth Lysons

Many people, for a variety of reasons, wish to continue in some form of paid employment after they have retired. This helpful guide explores the practical implications of such a choice and highlights some of the opportunities available.

£5.95 0–86242–103–9

Age and Employment: Why employers should think again about older workers
Richard Worsley

Aimed at employers, this thought-provoking new book invites them to think again about their present attitudes to and treatment of older employees – both in the interests of their own businesses and in the wider interests of the community and the economy. It draws on the Carnegie UK Trust's work on older workers, and material from employers, researchers and other institutions. It includes 29 case studies.

£14.95 0–86242–204–3

Preparing for Retirement: The employer's guide
Joanna Walker
The need to prepare staff for their retirement is widely accepted, yet many organisations fail to provide any training at all. This guide, designed to help personnel staff formulate a pre-retirement training policy, sets out the options available and the stages that need to be followed.
Co-published with the Pre-Retirement Association
£12.95 0–86242–068–7

Money matters

The Pensions Handbook: A mid-career guide
to improving retirement income
Sue Ward
This annual guide provides all the information people in mid-career need to improve their pension arrangements. The three main types of pension scheme – State, occupational and personal – are described in detail and guidance is provided on increasing their value. The options available when changing job, taking early retirement or carrying on working after pension age are examined in detail. There are special sections on pension issues for women. The book also addresses the position of those wrongly advised to buy personal pensions.
For further information please ring 0181-679 8000

Your Taxes and Savings: A guide for older people
Peta Hodge and Sally West
This definitive annual guide to financial planning provides a comprehensive explanation of the impact of taxation on the finances of older people. It also looks at managing retirement income and evaluates the wide range of investment opportunities available. Advice is given on building an investment portfolio and model portfolios are included.
For further information please ring 0181-679 8000.

Your Rights: A guide to money benefits for older people
Sally West
A highly successful annual guide to the State benefits available to older people. This edition includes details of the new Incapacity Benefit, which replaced Invalidity Benefit and Sickness Benefit on 13 April 1995, and of the new Jobseeker's Allowance, which replaces Unemployment

Benefit in October 1996. It also contains current information on other benefits for disabled people, retirement pensions, Income Support, Housing Benefit, Council Tax Benefit, and paying for residential care.
For further information please ring 0181-679 8000

The Insurance Handbook: A guide for older people
Wayne Asher
Older people have particular needs – and opportunities – when purchasing insurance. This practical guide provides a useful overview of the products on the market, including home and contents, car, holiday, health and life insurance. The aim is to help readers get value for money and find a product that is really right for their needs.
£6.95 0–86242–146–2

Health and care

Caring in a Crisis: Choices for the carer of an elderly relative
Marina Lewycka
Being a carer may mean many different things – from living at a distance and keeping a check on things by telephone to taking on a full-time caring role. This book looks at the choices facing someone whose parent or other relative needs care. It helps readers look at their own circumstances and their own priorities and decide what is the best role for themselves – as well as the person being cared for.
£6.95 0–86242–184–5

Caring in a Crisis: What to do and who to turn to
Marina Lewycka
At some point in their lives millions of people find themselves suddenly responsible for organising the care of an older person with a health crisis. All too often such carers have no idea what services are available or who can be approached for support. This book is designed to act as a first point of reference in just such an emergency, signposting readers on to many more detailed, local sources of advice.
£6.95 0–86242–136–5

Caring in a Crisis: Caring for someone who has dementia
Jane Brotchie
Caring for someone with dementia can be physically and emotionally exhausting, and it is often difficult to think about what can be done to

make the situation easier. This book shows how to cope and seek further help as well as containing detailed information on the illness itself and what to expect in the future.

£6.95 0–86242–182–9

Caring in a Crisis: Caring for someone who has had a stroke
Philip Coyne with Penny Mares
Although 100,000 people in Britain will have a stroke this year, many people are still confused about what stroke actually means. Supportive and positive, this book is designed to help carers understand stroke and its immediate aftermath. It contains extensive information on hospital discharge, providing care, rehabilitation and adjustment to life at home.

£6.95 0–86242–183–7

If you would like to order any of these titles, please write to the address below, enclosing a cheque or money order for the appropriate amount made payable to Age Concern England. Credit card orders may be made on 0181-679 8000.

Mail Order Unit
Age Concern England
PO Box 9
London SW16 4EX

Index